TUNE IN TO ENGLISH

Second Edition

Learning English Through Familiar Melodies

SingLing and LingoRap

Uwe Kind

Delta Publishing Company

DELTA PUBLISHING COMPANY
A Division of DELTA SYSTEMS COMPANY, INC.
1400 Miller Parkway
McHenry, IL 60050 USA
(815) 363–3582   Toll Free (800) 323–8270
www.delta–systems.com

Printed in the United States of America

10 9 8 7 6 5 4 3 2

Written by Uwe Kind

Illustrations by Yvette Kaplan

Text   1-887744-78-9
CD   1-887744-79-7

ABOUT THE AUTHOR

The inventor behind SingLing and LingoRap is Uwe Kind, president of Kind International.

Mr. Kind is an international communicator himself, having escaped from former East Germany to the West in 1960. As a German teacher at the New School in New York City, Mr. Kind developed SingLing, a language learning technique based on familiar tunes, which he later refined as a graduate student at Harvard University. Mr. Kind has since published four SingLing books—"O Susanne, ja konjugier für mich," "Eine kleine Deutschmusik," "Deutschvergnügen" and "Tune in to Español"—which are used by students and teachers worldwide as a fun and effective way to learn conversational German, Spanish, or English (as a second language).

Mr. Kind's approach extends well beyond the classroom. Some of his notable students include: Johnny Carson and David Letterman (he taught them to speak German and Chinese on their late night shows); Gail Sheehy (German); New York construction workers (taught them French on the 'Real People' TV show); Rykers island inmates (English) and correction officers (Spanish); Sesame Street's Big Bird (German), Harlem tour guides (German) and countless corporate executives.

In 1993 Mr. Kind was honored for his work at the prestigious 'Documenta', one of the world's premier modern art exhibitions. The work was selected as a prime example of the power of art in education.

Although he now travels extensively to train teachers and to hold LingoTech concerts here and abroad, Mr. Kind makes his home in New York City. It is only a matter of time before we see what else he dreams up to contribute to world understanding.

ACKNOWLEDGMENTS

I would like to express my appreciation to the students of The New School and Harvard University who encouraged me to write this text. Special thanks to Donna Swain of the New School University, Ursual Meyer and Peter Apelt of the Goethe Institut New York, Helene Zimmer Loew of the American Association of Teachers of German and Dr. Christa Kirby of Pinellas County Schools, who supported me with great enthusiasm in the early stages of my work. In addition I want to thank Dr. Aimee Leifer Dorr, Dr. Harry Lasker , and Dr. Maria Tatar of Harvard University and Mark Moersen of NBC TV for their help in guiding me in my research with SingLing and LingoRap.

Last but not least, my gratitude goes to the great artists and composers, known and unknown, whose artwork and music I was able to use in Tune In To English.

Uwe Kind

INTRODUCTION

Tune In To English, by using universally known melodies with new lyrics, helps students review idiomatic expressions, vocabulary, and structures while learning practical English language functions. The songs facilitate the learning process through the use of rhyme, rhythm, and familiar tunes.

Tune In To English has been designed as a supplementary text primarily for the high school or adult student of English as a second language at a beginning or intermediate level; however, it can be used by ESL students of all ages. The book is divided into 22 units, with two additional review units. Each unit includes one song preceded by a brief introduction describing the situation on which the new lyrics are based. The songs are of two types: dialogue songs and narrative songs. They each teach a specific language function such as introducing oneself, asking for directions, or making a purchase. This is followed by a musical score with guitar chords and the verses. Since all of the songs in **Tune In To English** are internationally known, the book can also be used effectively without the audio CD. Music and guitar chords are provided in the text for teachers and/or students who play a musical instrument. However, musical accompaniment is not necessary and the songs can be equally successful with the help of some enthusiastic singers.

The language in each song is reviewed through a series of challenging games, exercises, puzzles, and other various activities. These activities encourage students to apply the material they have learned in different situations. The review sections after units 11 and 22 contain exercises to reinforce material taught in previous units. Detailed instructions and suggestions on how to use the songs are given in the section titled To the Teacher.

An answer key and an index of structures are provided at the back of the book. The answer key gives the answers to all exercises and the solutions to all puzzles in the text. The index of structures makes it possible to locate songs which provide practice for a particular grammatical point.

THE SINGLING AND LINGORAP METHOD

The idea that music can affect one's body is not new. It has been found that music can influence the rhythm of breathing, and thus relax the body, heightening awareness and mental receptivity. For centuries important information has been memorized and passed on through songs and poetry.

The SingLing and LingoRap are based on these findings. They use familiar tunes to teach language. The familiarity of the tunes creates a satisfying feeling of recognition, which helps to overcome the fear of and resistance to the unknown that the student may experience.

This method has been developed and tested by the author at Harvard University and at The New School for Social Research in New York. It has also been tested with impressive results at several other American and European schools. It has been found that foreign languages can be taught more effectively and rapidly, and with greater recall, through the use of songs rather than mechanical classroom drills.

Even students who are tone deaf can learn more through rhythmic reciting of the song verses or by merely listening, because the enjoyable melodies and rhythms put them in a receptive mood. Transition from singing to speaking is a natural process since the verses conserve spoken inflection and pronunciation. Because of its enormous learning potential, SingLing and LingoRap are being used in many schools and universities in the United States.

TO THE TEACHER

Before beginning **Tune In To English**, give the student a brief explanation of SingLing and LingoRap. Point out that rhyme, rhythm, and a familiar melody aid in learning and remembering. Since important elements of this method are relaxation and enjoyment, students should not be compelled to sing. Those who claim they cannot sing or are too shy to do so should listen to the others. The second time the class sings the song, suggest that those who didn't sing the first time recite the words rhythmically. Quite often students, who at first refuse to sing, eventually join in because they do not wish to be left out or because they realize that singing is not so difficult. Stress the fact that listening, rhythmic speaking, or mental singing are equally effective and that a good voice is not required. Once singing is under way, your students will realize how enjoyable it is and how quickly they can learn.

Tune In To English can be used at the beginning of a class to create a relaxed atmosphere, during class to provide a bridge between different activities and a change of pace, or at the end of the class to finish on an upbeat note. The following steps can be followed for each unit:

1. Have the students open to the first page of the unit, read the title, and look at the picture. Ask them to explain what they think is taking place in the picture. Then have them look at the name of the tune and, if someone has recognized it, ask that person to hum it.

2. Play the audio CD. Have the students listen to the introduction to the song as they read it in their books. If the CD is not available, read the introduction aloud to the students.

3. The speaker on the CD will then instruct the students to listen to the song. He or she will teach the song by asking the students to sing the different parts one at a time. Finally, the students will sing the entire song along with the singers on the CD. If the CD is not available, sing the song to the class. Sing it a second time, having the students repeat each line after you. Then have them sing the entire song together. Divide the class into groups and have each group sing a different part of the song. In the case of the dialogue songs, each group will sing a different character's part. In the case of the narrative songs, each group will sing a different verse.

4. After teaching the song, have the students complete the exercises. They should check their answers in the answer key at the back of the book.

TO THE STUDENT

Tune In To English can be used for self–instruction. Follow these steps for each unit:

1. Open to the first page of the unit, read the title, and look at the picture. Describe what you think is taking place in the picture. Look at the name of the tune and, if you have recognized it, try to hum it.

2. Play the audio CD. Listen to the introduction to the song as you read it in your book.

3. Listen to the song as often as possible, and relax while listening. The speaker on the tape will teach the song by asking you to sing the different parts one at a time. Finally, sing the entire song with the singers on the CD.

4. After singing the song several times, do the exercises. Check your answers in the answer key at the back of the book.

After using **Tune In To English**, structures which you may have found difficult will come to mind in seconds if you simply try to recall the particular tune.

Table of Contents

Tune In To English

1 *I'm Glad To Meet You*

It's a cold winter day in New York. Alice is standing on a windy street waiting for a bus. She notices a tourist next to her. He's carrying a little suitcase covered with stickers from all over South America. She decides to start a conversation.

Tune: La Cucaracha
Mexican folk song

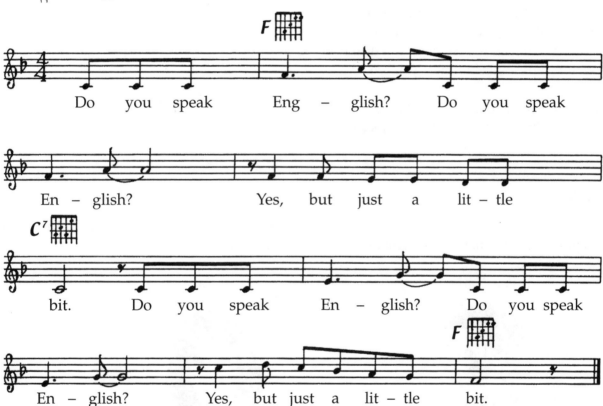

Do you speak Eng – glish? Do you speak

En – glish? Yes, but just a lit – tle

bit. Do you speak En – glish? Do you speak

En – glish? Yes, but just a lit – tle bit.

Verses

  Alice: Do you speak English? Do you speak English?
Victor: Yes, but just a little bit.
  Alice: Do you speak English? Do you speak English?
Victor: Yes, but just a little bit.

Alice: Are you from Chile? Are you from Chile?
Victor: No, I'm not. I'm from Brazil.
Alice: Are you from Chile? Are you from Chile?
Victor: No, I'm not. I'm from Brazil.

Victor: My name is Victor. My name is Victor.
What's your name and where're you from?
My name is Victor. My name is Victor.
What's your name and where're you from?

Alice: My name is Alice. My name is Alice.
I'm from Washington, D.C.
My name is Alice. My name is Alice.
I'm from Washington, D.C.

Alice: I'm glad to meet you. I'm glad to meet you.
Victor: I'm so glad to meet you too.
Alice: I'm glad to meet you. I'm glad to meet you.
Victor: I'm so glad to meet you too.

Alice and Victor decide to go and see New York together. They walk along Fifth Avenue, have lunch in Chinatown, and then visit the Statue of Liberty.

Jumbles

Alice is introducing Victor to some other tourists that she knows. But she has the names of their countries and languages all mixed up. Can you help her straighten them out?

This is Mario.

LITAY

He's from _____.

LATILAN

He speaks _____.

This is Katsura.

PANJA

She's from _____.

SEPAJENA

She speaks _____.

This is Monique.

CENFRA

She's from _____.

CHEFRN

She speaks _____.

This is Geraldo.

RIZABL

He's from _____.

GETOPURSUE

He speaks _____.

This is Uwe and this is Ulla.

MGYARNE

They're from _____.

ENGMAR

They speaks _____.

This is Carlos and this is Maria.

OXIMEC

They're from _____.

NASPISH

They speaks _____.

Grammarhyme

Fill in the blanks with the word or expression from the right that rhymes.

Example:

Hello, Mrs. Vanish   Spanish

Do you speak <u>Spanish</u>?   English

I'm from London. My name's Tom Thumb.   how've you been

What's your name and _____?   where're you from

Are you Mr. Jerry Spot?   Yes, I am

_____.   No, I'm not

This is Mrs. Lucy Bell.   very well

She speaks English _____.   and French

How do you do?   be your friend

I'm glad _____.   to meet you

This is Mrs. Linda Austin.   Boston

Mrs. Austin is from_____.   San Francisco

This is Mr. Freddy Freeze.   German

He speaks English and _____.   Japanese

Balloons

Complete the balloons using the hints below. Then sing your new song.

1. English
3. Moscow
4. Peru

5. Sylvia
7. Elvis
   Nashville, Tennessee

2 There's a Little Grocery Store Right Across the Street

It's five o'clock on Saturday afternoon. Rose is planning a party for tonight. The stores will be closing in one hour and Rose doesn't know where to go shopping. She tells her friend Pete what she needs, and he tells her where to go.

Tune: Row, Row, Row Your Boat
American folk song

I need sal - ad, Pete. I need sal - ad, Pete.

There's a lit - tle gro - cery store right a - cross the street.

Verses

Rose: I need salad, Pete.
I need salad, Pete.
Pete: There's a little grocery store
right across the street.

Rose: I need lamb chops, Pete.
I need lamb chops, Pete.
Pete: There's a little butcher shop
right across the street.

Rose: I need pastry, Pete.
I need pastry, Pete.
Pete: There's a little pastry shop
right across the street.

Rose: I need flowers, Pete.
I need flowers, Pete.
Pete: There's a little florist shop
right across the street.

Rose: I need aspirin, Pete.
I need aspirin, Pete.
Pete: There's a little pharmacy
right across the street.

Complete

Use the pictures to complete the following sentences.

Example:

Where can I get some <u>pastry</u>, Pete?

There's a <u>pastry shop</u> across the street.

Where can I get some _____, Pete?

There's a _____ across the street.

Where can I get some _____, Pete?

There's a _____ across the street.

I need some _____, Pete.

There's a _____ across the street.

I need some _____, Pete.

There's a _____ across the street.

Where can I get some _____, Pete?

There's a _____ across the street.

Where can I get some _____, Pete?

There's a _____ across the street.

Match

Here are the things Rose wants to buy. Draw lines to match the objects with the stores and you'll see where Rose went shopping.

Puzzles

To solve these picture puzzles, you must spell the words that the objects stand for, add and subtract the proper letters, and then unscramble them. The boxes at the bottom of each puzzle show how many letters the answer has.

3 *How Much Is It?*

Do you like to hagel? Do you like to get a bargain? If you do, then this song may save you a couple of dollars. Listen and figure out if the lady gets the deal she's looking for.

Tune: Lingo Rap

Verses

Lady: How much is it, sir?
How much does it sell for?
How much is it sir?
How much does it cost?

Lady: How much is it, sir?
How much does it sell for?

Salesman: Ninety–five dollars!
It's a very good price!

Refrain: Eighty one, eighty two,
eighty three, eighty four, eighty
five, eighty six, eighty seven,
eighty eight, eighty nine, ninety?

Lady: That's expensive, sir!
That is more than I thought!

Salesman: That's a very good price!
That's a very good deal!
It's a very good price!
It's a very good deal!

Lady: I don't want to spend that much!
Thank you very much. Good bye!

Refrain: Eighty one, eighty two, eighty three,
eighty four, eighty five, eighty six
eighty seven, eighty eight, eighty
nine, ninety?

Salesman: I will take eighty five,
if you pay me in cash.

Lady: All I have is eighty two.

Salesman: Alright, eighty two for you.

Refrain: Eighty one, eighty two, eighty three,
eighty four, eighty five, eighty six,
eighty seven, eighty eight, eighty
nine, ninety?

Grammarhyme

Complete the rhyme with one of the words on the right side. Write the words in the blanks.

Example:

Mrs. Bisset,

<u>how much is it?</u>

how are you?
How much does it cost?
how much is it?

Now I'm lost!

_____

Where am I?
How much does it cost?
Please help me!

Ms. Hutch,

_____

how are you?
how much does it cost?
I don't want to spend that much.

Oh, Neal, let's buy it.

_____

It's such a good deal.
It's a very good price.
I like it.

This is nice

_____

and attractive.
and not expensive.
and a very good price.

Ms. Ash, can you

_____

give me eighty one dollars?
me in cash?
wait a moment?

How much is your fee?

_____

Eighty nine.
Eighty four.
Eighty three.

I want that door.

_____

How much is it?
How much does it sell for?
How much does it cost?

Write A New Dialog

Put the following sentences in the right order.

I will take it for thirty two.

I don't want to spend that much.

Forty two dollars? That's more than I thought!

Good bye.

How much is this CD player?

Hello!

All I have is thirty two dollars.

This CD player here is forty two dollars.

Hello. May I help you?

It's a very good price.

How much can you spend?

Alright, thirty two for you.

Thank you. Good bye.

1. _____

2. _____

3. _____

4. _____

5. _____

6. _____

7. _____

8. _____

9. _____

10. _____

11. _____

12. _____

13. _____

Match

What do you say when...? Draw a line to the item in the right column that answers the question in the left.

What do you say when you want to know the price?   That's a good deal.

What do you say when something is too expensive?   That's expensive.

What do you say when something nice costs very little?   How much is it?

What do you say when you're on a low budget?   How much does it sell for?

How do you ask for a price of an item?   That's more than I thought.

4 My Father Has A Sister

Patricia Grant is my aunt. She has three children: Peter, Paul, and Mary. Peter, Paul, and Mary are my cousins. Their father's name is Patrick Grant. He's my uncle. Aunt Patricia also has a brother. His name is Chris.

Tune: Oh, My Darling Clementine
American folk song

Well, my fa - ther has a sis - ter and her name's Pa - tri - cia Grant, and her chil - dren are my cous - ins and their mo - ther is my aunt.

Verses

Well, my father has a sister
and her name's Patricia Grant,
and her children are my cousins
and their mother is my aunt.

Well, my father has a sister
and her name's Patricia Grant,
and her husband is my uncle
and his wife, well, that's my aunt.

Well, my father has a sister
and her name's Patricia Grant,
and her brother is my father
and his sister is my aunt.

And my aunt has got a brother,
and her brother's name is Chris,
and his wife, well, that's my mother.
Can you tell me who Chris is?

Solve the puzzle on page 15 to find out who Chris is.

 Tune In To English

Puzzle

Find out who Chris is. Complete the clues and write the words horizontally in the blank spaces of the puzzle. You'll find the answer in the gray column.

Verse I: Well, **1.** _____ father has a sister

and her name's Patricia Grant

and her children are my **2.** _____

and **4.** _____ mother is my **3.** _____ .

Verse III: Well, my **5.** _____ has a sister

and her name's Patricia **6.** _____ ,

and her **7.** _____ is my **8.** _____

and their mother is my aunt.

Verse IV: And my aunt has got a brother

and **9.** _____ brother's name is Chris,

and his wife, well, that's my **10.** _____

Can you tell me who Chris is?

Family Circle

Check the box next to the appropriate answer.

1. My grandmother has one child, a daughter. Who is my grandmother's daughter?

   ☐ a. Your sister

   ☐ b. Your mother

   ☐ c. Your cousin

   ☐ d. Your father

2. John's aunt Mary has one brother and no sisters. Who is aunt Mary's brother?

   ☐ a. John's friend

   ☐ b. John's father

   ☐ c. John's brother

   ☐ d. John's grandfather

3. Maria's aunt has a daughter Her. name is Sylvia. Who is Sylvia?

   ☐ a. Maria's aunt

   ☐ b. Maria's uncle

   ☐ c. Maria's sister

   ☐ d. Maria's cousin

4. Donald's grandfather has two children, Ted and Bill. Bill is Donald's uncle. Who is Ted?

   ☐ a. Donald's father

   ☐ b. Donald's friend

   ☐ c. Donald's mother

   ☐ d. Donald's brother

5. Ted's mother has a daughter. Her name is Judy. Who is Judy?

   ☐ a. Ted's brother

   ☐ b. Ted's aunt

   ☐ c. Ted's sister

   ☐ d. Ted's girlfriend

6. Judy's mother has a sister. Her name is Polly. Who is Polly?

   ☐ a. Judy's aunt

   ☐ b. Judy's cousin

   ☐ c. Judy's uncle

   ☐ d. Judy's grandmother

Balloons

Complete the balloons to find out whose car this is.

5 First Turn Right At The Light

Greenwich Village is a little city within the big city of New York. Many of New York City's artists live in the Village. It's a beautiful area. But its many small streets often confuse people. André is from France but he's in New York this month and he wants to visit his friend in the Village. He asks a young woman named Carolyn for directions.

Tune: Sur Le Pont
French folk song

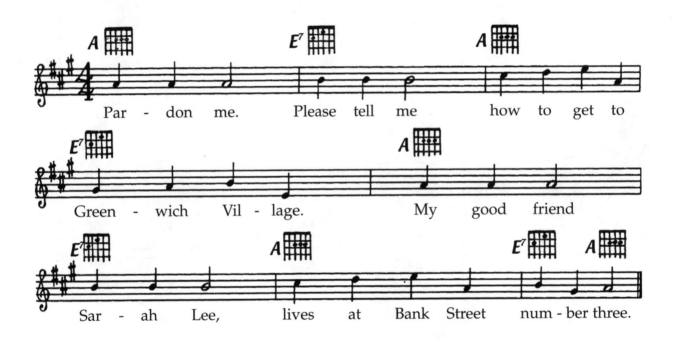

Par - don me. Please tell me how to get to Green - wich Vil - lage. My good friend Sar - ah Lee, lives at Bank Street num - ber three.

Verses

André: Pardon me. Please tell me
how to get to Greenwich Village.
My good friend, Sarah Lee,
lives at Bank Street number three.

Carolyn: First turn right at the light,
walk two blocks, stop at the corner.
Then turn left at the zoo.
That is Greenwich Avenue.
Walk two blocks straight ahead,

Tune In To English

pass the school and pass the market.
Then turn left at the store.
That's the street you're looking for.

André: Now I know where to go.
I'll just follow your directions.
Thanks so much, now I'm fine.

Carolyn: You're quite welcome. Any time.

Grammarhyme

Complete each sentence of the rhyme with one of the words on the right. Write the words in the blanks.

Example:

Pardon, Lee. Please tell <u>me</u>.	him me
Pardon, sir. Please tell _____ how to get to downtown London.	me her
Her friends Sam and Sara Shore live at South Street number _____.	four three
First turn right at the _____.	bank light
Pass the pool, and pass the _____.	drugstore school
Pass the old wall, pass the _____.	town hall ballpark
Pass the bench in front of the store, and that is South Street number _____.	eight four

CHAPTER 5: FIRST TURN RIGHT AT THE LIGHT

Balloons

Martin is visiting New York. He's standing on the corner of 14th Street and Sixth Avenue. He wants to visit his friend who lives at 4 East 12th Street. He stops a woman to ask for directions.

Complete the balloons. Refer back to the song if you need help. Use the map below for pictures three and four.

Giving Directions

Rachel wants to walk to school this morning. Since she usually takes the bus, she's not sure which way to walk. Can you give her the right directions? Follow the arrows on the map and write sentences to tell her which way to go.

_____

_____

_____

_____

_____

_____

_____

6 Merry Christmas

Christmas is an important holiday in many countries. It's a time for giving and receiving gifts. In the United States many children believe that it's a person called "Santa Claus" who brings the gifts. He lives at the North Pole, and on the night before Christmas he delivers gifts to children all over the world in a sleigh pulled by eight reindeer. So children often send letters to Santa to tell him what they want for Christmas. Here's a letter from Tommy Tuttle.

Tune: This Old Man
Traditional American song

Bring her gloves for the cold. Bring her ear-rings
made of gold Bring her choc-o-late,
can-dy canes, and nuts. Bring her mon-ney, bring her lots.

Verses

For Mother:
Bring her gloves for the cold.
Bring her earrings made of gold.
Bring her chocolate, candy canes, and nuts.
Bring her money, bring her lots.

For me:
Bring me boots for the rain.
Bring me cars for my old train.
Bring me chocolate, candy canes, and nuts.
Bring me money, bring me lots.

For Father:
Bring him ties for his suits.
Bring him leather cowboy boots.
Bring him chocolate, candy canes, and nuts.
Bring him money, bring him lots.

For us all:
Bring us snow. Bring us ice.
A white Christmas would be nice.
Bring us health and happiness and love.
Merry Christmas. That's enough.

Word Hunt

Tom and his family will find 30 gifts under the tree on Christmas morning. The names of the gifts listed below are hidden in the box. Find them by reading forward, up, down, or diagonally. Circle each word as you find it. The first word is circled to give you a start.

train	pipe	watch
coat	money	bat
shoes	toys	ball
boots	socks	hat
candy	pen	ring
nuts	books	cat
shirt	gloves	scarf
doll	suit	radio
skirt	earrings	kite
pants	wallet	record

s	t	e	m	q	r	s	o	c	k	s	e
a	g	a	s	k	i	r	t	a	a	k	w
c	l	s	h	o	e	s	h	n	w	t	a
r	o	u	i	a	r	c	i	d	o	l	l
m	v	i	r	s	t	a	x	y	l	c	l
o	e	t	t	u	r	r	d	a	z	f	e
u	s	n	u	t	s	f	b	i	b	a	t
w	a	t	c	h	y	r	e	c	o	r	d
p	i	p	e	t	d	g	b	o	o	k	s
e	r	i	n	g	o	c	o	a	t	i	p
n	j	m	o	n	e	y	v	t	s	t	l
e	a	r	r	i	n	g	s	o	r	e	i

Balloons

Study the pictures. Select the answer to the question from the choices given and write it in the balloon.

What is the woman saying to the waiter?

> a. Bring him a knife, please.
> b. Bring him the salt, please.
> c. Bring him the pepper, please.

What is the woman saying to the clerk?

> a. Give her an envelope for her letter.
> b. Give her a pen, please.
> c. Give her a stamp, please.

What is the girl saying to her father?

> a. Buy me a picture for my room.
> b. Buy me a chair for my table.
> c. Buy me a bed for my room.

Make a Wish

Imagine that you have found an old bottle in your basement. You open it and out pops a genie who promises to bring you any six objects you wish. Choose three from the picture below and make up three of your own. Write the names of the objects in the spaces at the bottom of the page.

Please bring me…

1._____   4. _____

2. _____   5. _____

3. _____   6. _____

7 Copycat

Peter has a cat named Jenny. She admires Peter very much. She follows him everywhere, and copies everything that he does. She's a real "copycat." Listen to what Peter has to say about Jenny.

Tune: She'll Be Comin' 'Round The Mountain
Traditional American song

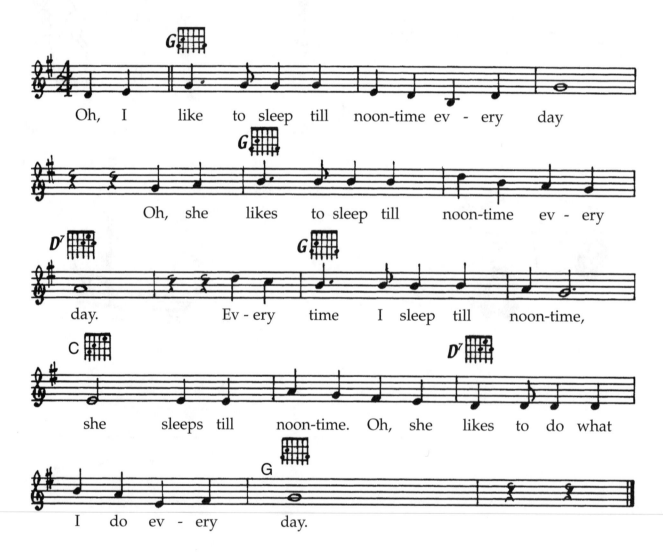

Oh, I like to sleep till noon-time ev - ery day

Oh, she likes to sleep till noon-time ev - ery

day. Ev - ery time I sleep till noon-time,

she sleeps till noon-time. Oh, she likes to do what

I do ev - ery day.

Tune In To English

Verses

Oh, I like to sleep till noontime every day.
Oh, she likes to sleep till noontime every day.
Every time I sleep till noontime, she sleeps till noontime.
Oh, she likes to do what I do every day.

Oh, I like to take a shower every day.
Oh, she likes to take a shower every day.
Every time I take a shower, she takes a shower.
Oh, she likes to do what I do every day.

Oh, I like to do a headstand every day.
Oh, she likes to do a headstand every day.
Every time I do a headstand, she does a headstand.
Oh, she likes to do what I do every day.

Oh, I like to study English every day.
Oh, she likes to study English every day.
Every time I study English, she studies English.
Oh, she likes to do what I do every day.

Fill-Ins

What do you like to do? What don't you like to do? Fill in the blanks to make your own list.

I like to _____.

I like to _____.

I also like to _____.

I don't like to _____.

I don't like to _____.

I don't like to _____ either.

Answer the Questions

Go over the song. Then answer the questions.

Example:

Does Jenny like to get up at seven every day?
<u>No, Jenny doesn't like to get up at seven every day.</u>

Does Jenny like to take a bath every day?

_____ .

Does Jenny like to study English every day?

_____ .

Does Jenny like to do a headstand every day?

_____ .

Does Jenny like to take a shower every day?

_____ .

Does Jenny like to sleep till noon every day?

_____ .

Balloons

Peter also has a dog. His name is Broom because he looks like a broom. What does Broom like to do every day? Choose the correct answer and write it in Peter's balloon.

1. a. He likes to play ball every day.

b. He likes to watch TV every day.

c. He likes to take a bath every day.

2.   a. Broom likes to drink milk every day.

     b. Broom likes to eat a banana every day.

     c. Broom likes to drink water every day.

3.   a. Broom likes to read every day.

     b. Broom likes to do a headstand every day.

     c. Broom likes to dance every day.

4.   a. Broom likes to ride in my car every day.

     b. Broom likes to run in the park every day.

     c. Broom likes to sing every day.

5.   a. He likes to take a nap every day.

     b. He likes to learn to speak every day.

     c. He likes to take a shower every day.

8 I Feel Happy Today

Do you feel "up" at times and "down" at other times? Sometimes it's the weather that influences your mood. Sometimes it's the day of the week. Sometimes you're in a good mood and you don't know why. Susan works in an office from Monday to Friday. On Monday she's usually in a bad mood. On Friday she usually feels happy because the weekend has arrived. Let's see how she felt this week.

Tune: Good Morning
Traditional American song

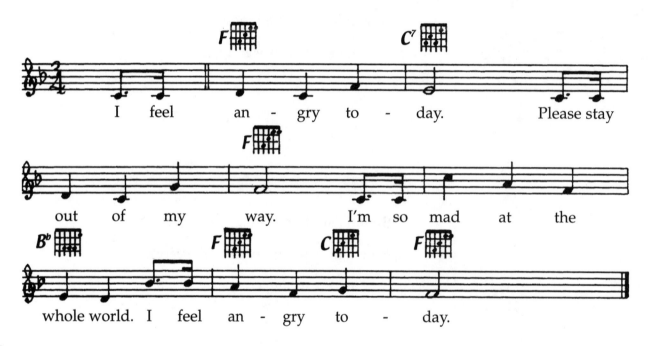

I feel an - gry to - day. Please stay out of my way. I'm so mad at the whole world. I feel an - gry to - day.

Verses

On Monday:
I feel angry today.
Please stay out of my way.
I'm so mad at the whole world.
I feel angry today.

On Tuesday:
I feel terribly blue.
I don't know what to do.
'Cause it's cold and it's raining.
I feel terribly blue.

On Thursday:
I feel nervous and tense.
It just doesn't make sense.
I can't take all this pressure.
I feel nervous and tense.

On Friday:
I feel happy today.
It's been sunny all day.
And I don't work tomorrow.
I feel happy today.

Tune In To English

Grammarhyme

Complete the rhyme by filling in the blank spaces. If you need help, go back to the song on page 29.

This is Mr. Zappy.

He's feeling very _____.

It's been sunny all day.

He feels happy _____.

This is Judy Spence.

At work she's nervous and c

Judy's boss, Jane Fence,

thinks it doesn't make much _____.

This is Miss Peekaboo.

She feels terribly _____.

She tells her cat Sue

that she doesn't know what _____.

This is Mrs. Langry.

Today she feels quite _____.

She's had a bad day,

so stay out of her _____.

Chapter# Chapter 8: I Feel Happy Today

Write

Write a sentence about how you usually feel at these times.

    1. How do you feel when the sun shines?

_____

_____

    2. How do you feel when it rains?

_____

_____

    3. How do you feel when you have to take a test?

_____

_____

    4. How do you feel when you're at a party?

_____

_____

    5. How do you feel when someone you're supposed to meet is late?

_____

_____

Balloons

How do they feel today? Answer the question in the balloon on the left and write it in the balloon on the right.

How do you feel today?

How do you

feel today?

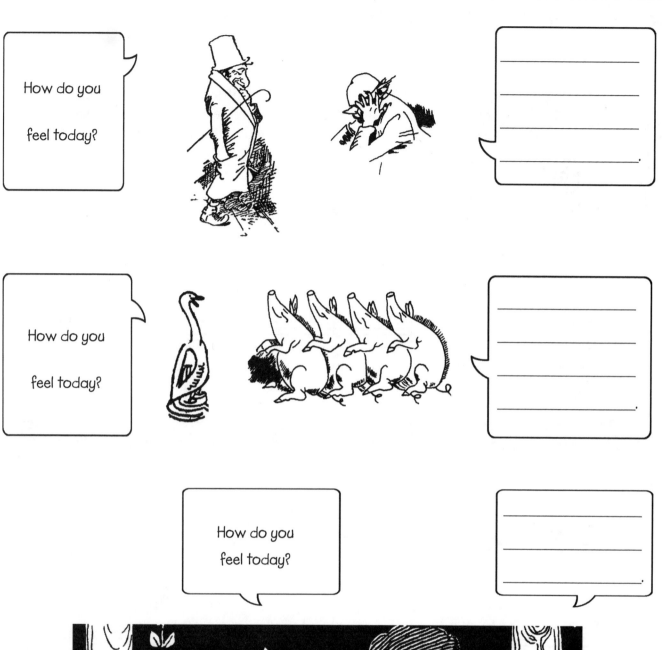

How do you

feel today?

How do you

feel today?

9 In Front Of My House There's A Tree

Dan Duncan lives in a little house in the country. It's an ideal house, because it's near a hill, a creek, a lake, and a park. Let's listen to him tell more about his house.

Tune: Chapanecas
Mexican folk song

In front of my house there's a tree my cat likes to climb it with me. In back of my house there's a hill where I go hik-ing with Bill.

TUNE IN TO ENGLISH

Verses

In front of my house there's a tree.
My cat likes to climb it with me.
In back of my house there's a hill
where I go hiking with Bill.

Next to my house there's a creek
where I catch fish every week.
Across the road there's a lake
where I go swimming with Jake.

Near my house there's a park.
I never go there after dark.
Around my house there's a lawn.
On weekends I sit there till dawn.

On top of my house there's a nest.
The bird living there is a pest.
Under the porch there's a mouse.
Sometimes it comes in the house.

Over the door there's a light.
It helps you to find me at night.
Inside my house there's lots more.
To see it just knock at my door.

Draw

Draw a picture by following the instructions below.

◯ circle   —— line   △ triangle   ▢ square

1. Draw a horizontal line.
2. Draw a big square on top of the line.
3. Draw a small square in the middle of the big one. Put it on top of the horizontal line.
4. Draw two small squares in the upper part of the big square.
5. Draw a triangle on top of the big square. The top line of the square should be the base of the triangle.
6. Draw a circle next to the triangle.
7. Draw short lines coming out of the circle.

What did you draw? Solution on page 96.

Balloons

Study each picture. Then choose an appropriate sentence and write it in the balloon.

1. a. On top of my house there's a lake.

    b. In front of my house there's a tree.

    c. In back of my house there's a tree.

2. a. There's a lamp in back of my sofa.

    b. There's a lamp under my sofa.

    c. There's a lamp next to my sofa.

3. a. My cat sleeps on top of my bed.

    b. My cat sleeps next to my bed.

    c. My cat sleeps under my bed.

Fill-Ins

Study the picture; then fill in the blanks.

1. There's a dog _____ the table.

2. There's a mouse _____ the table.

3. There's a cat _____ the table.

4. There's a chair _____ the table.

5. There's a frog _____ the chair.

6. There's a cake _____ the table.

7. There's a candle _____ the cake.

10 *Wrong Number*

Joe Monroe lives in Indiana and his girlfriend Diana lives in Oklahoma. He really wants to talk to her, but he's at work and he doesn't have her telephone number with him. He feels quite sure that her "area code"—the special number for her section of the country—is 406. And he thinks that her telephone number is 555–5342, or maybe 555–4352, or maybe 555–4253. He dials all three numbers, and each time he reaches a different place in Montana! Can you figure out what he's doing wrong?

Tune: Cielito Lindo
Mexican waltz

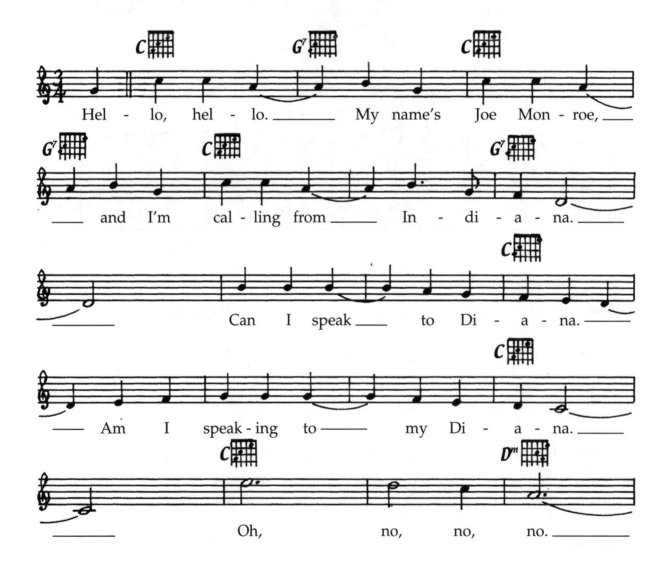

TUNE IN TO ENGLISH

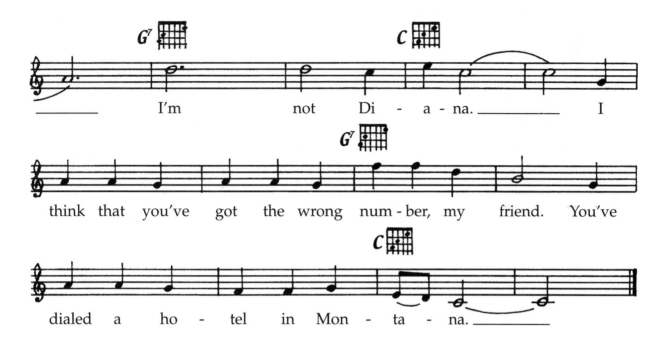

I'm not Di - a - na. _____ I think that you've got the wrong num - ber, my friend. You've dialed a ho - tel in Mon - ta - na. _____

Verses

Joe: Hello, hello.
My name's Joe Monroe,
and I'm calling from Indiana.
Can I speak to Diana, please?
Am I speaking to my Diana?

Party: Oh, no, no, no.
I'm not Diana
I think that you've got the
wrong number, my friend.
You've dialed a hotel in
Montana.

Joe: (I'd better try a different
number. He dials again.)

Joe: Hello, hello.
My name's Joe Monroe,
and I'm calling from Indiana.
Can I speak to Diana, please?
Am I speaking to my Diana?

Party: Oh, no, no, no.
I'm not Diana.
I think that you've got the
wrong number, my friend.
You've dialed a garage in Montana.

Joe: (I can't believe it! I've done it
again! He dials another number.)

Joe: Hello, hello.
My name's Joe Monroe,
and I'm calling from Indiana.
Can I speak to Diana, please?
Am I speaking to my Diana?

Party: Oh, no, no, no.
I'm not Diana.
I think that you've got the
wrong number, my friend.
You've dialed a cafe in
Montana.

Joe: (Not again! I give up!)

Now solve the puzzles on page 40 to find out what Joe's problem is.

Grammarhyme

Complete the rhyme. Choose the appropriate word from the right and write it in the blank.

I'm calling from Rome.   home
Is Mrs. Yellow _____.   there

Sorry, Mr. Fellow.   Yellow
This is not Mrs. _____.   Fleming

My name's Betty Lumber.   number
You have the wrong _____.   person

I'd like to talk to Lynn.   here
She's not _____.   in

Puzzles

To find out why Joe got the wrong number each time he dialed, solve these puzzles and write your answers in the boxes.

Balloons

Write a question in the bubble on the left and answer it in the bubble on the right. If you need help, go over the song on page 38.

11 Greetings From Italy

It's summertime and Mel is spending his vacation by the sea in Southern Italy. He's going swimming and diving and he has a nice tan. But he has a little problem, too. So he's sending this postcard to his sister Susannah in Savannah, Georgia. Let's find out what Mel's problem is.

Tune: Oh, Susannah!
American folk song
by Stephen Foster

My _____ dear Su - san - nah, how are you? I'm
hav - ing lots of fun. I _____ swim a lot and
have a tan from sit - ting in the sun.
Oh, Su - san - nah! I love the blue, blue
sea. Say hel - lo to ev - ery - one, and
lots of love from me.

TUNE IN TO ENGLISH

Verses

My dear Susannah, how are you?
I'm having lots of fun.
I swim a lot and have a tan
from sitting in the sun.

Oh, Susannah!
I love the blue, blue sea.
Say hello to everyone,
and lots of love from me.

The weather here is beautiful.
It hasn't rained one day.
I'm even learning how to dive
for lobster in the bay.

Oh, Susannah!
I love the blue, blue sea.
Say hello to everyone
and lots of love from me.

I lost my wallet yesterday
in front of the hotel.
Please send me money right away
and promise you won't tell.

Oh, Susannah!
I love the blue, blue sea.
Say hello to everyone
and lots of love from me.

Grammarhyme

Complete the sentences of the rhyme with the correct words from the right.

My dear Susannah, how are you?	time
I'm having lots of _____.	fun
Just yesterday I got sunstroke	sun
from sleeping in the _____.	bed
The weather here's been beautiful.	week
It's only rained all _____.	over
My stomach doesn't like the food	bad
and nothing here is _____.	cheap
Oh, Susannah!	sea
I hate the blue, blue _____.	sun
I hope I'll see you all real soon.	Bill
Sincerely, your friend _____.	Lee

Jumbles

Freddy has just received a letter from his friends Philip and Robert. They're on vacation. To find out where they're staying, unscramble the missing words and write them in the blank spaces. Check your answers on page 102; then sing your new song.

Our dearest _____, how are you?
(dyrdef)

We're _____, as you can see.
(nefi)

Right now we're spending _____ nice weeks
(rheet)

in northern _____.
(yregmna)

Oh, dear _____!
(eryfdd)

Regards from _____.
(gayernm)

Say _____ to all our friends,
(olehl)

and to your _____.
(lfiyma)

Although the weather's _____ cold
(ryev)

we go out _____ day.
(rveey)

We're meeting lots of _____ here.
(loeppe)

Don't know how long we'll _____.
(ayts)

Oh, _____ Freddy!
(rdae)

Regards from _____.
(myeagrn)

Give our love to all our _____
(drfsein)

and to _____ family.
(uoyr)

Greetings

Send a postcard to anyone you wish. Choose from the information below. Then fill out the postcard.

Dear	How are you? I'm	I need	This place is
mom/dad	fine	more money	exciting
friend's name	sick	my camera	boring
Mr./Mrs./Miss/Ms.	Bored	company	expensive
		a lot of fun	
		full of nice people	

The weather is	I think about you	I hope you are	Give my best to
awful	every day	well	everyone
wonderful	often	happy	our friends
		the family	
		Mr./Mrs./Miss/Ms.	

Lots of love/Best wishes/Sincerely
(your name)

Dear _____,

   How are you? I'm _____.

I need _____.

This place is _____.

The weather is _____.

I think about you _____.

I hope you are _____.

Give my best to _____.

     _____,

     _____

Review

Detective

Can you detect what's wrong with each of these song lines? Write the correct lines in the spaces provided. Refer to the songs if you need help.

1. Do you speak English? Yes, but not today.

_____

_____

2. I need flowers, Pete. There's a little butcher shop right across the street.

_____

_____

3. My father has a brother and her name's Patricia Grant.

_____

_____

4. First turn right at the moon, walk two blocks, stop at the corner.

_____

_____

5. Bring her gloves for her toes. Bring her earrings for her nose.

_____

_____

6. Every time I take a shower, she takes a bath. Oh, she likes to do what I do every day.

_____

_____

7. I feel nervous today. It's been sunny all day.

_____

_____

8. On top of my house there's a lawn. On weekends I fish there till dawn.

_____

_____

9. I think that you've got the wrong planet, my friend. You've written a garage in Montana.

_____

_____

10. I lost my monkey yesterday in front of the hotel. Please send me money right away.

_____

_____

Jumbles

If you rearrange the words in each line, you'll have a sentence from one of your songs. Write the correct sentence and the name of the tune it's from.

1. you your and from what's are name where

_____

_____

2. the across a there's street pharmacy little right

_____

_____

3. me who you tell can is Chris

_____

_____

4. how me please to to tell Village get Greenwich

_____

_____

5. nuts me canes and chocolate bring candy

_____

_____

6. time noontime I every sleeps sleep she till noontime till

_____

_____

7. whole so I'm the mad world at

_____

_____

8. with I where across lake a road Jake swimming the there's go

_____

_____

9. from name's Monroe calling Indiana my Joe and I'm

_____

_____

10. everyone love of lots and hello to me from say

_____

_____

12 *I'm Looking For A Raincoat*

It's summer, the end of July. Hector is from sunny Spain. He's visiting San Francisco this month. It's raining and it's cold there. Hector didn't bring any clothes for this kind of weather, so he's gone to a clothing store to buy a raincoat and sweater. He's talking to the clerk right now.

Tune: Frère Jacques
Traditional French song

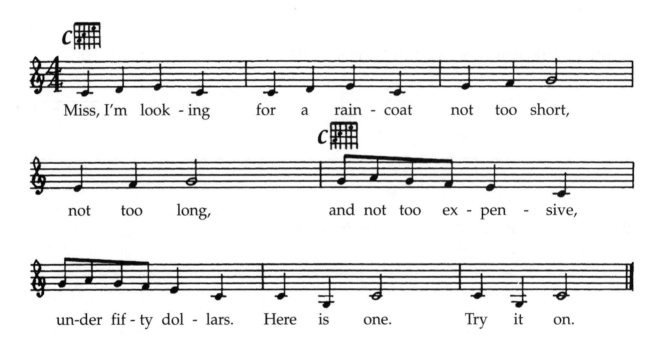

Miss, I'm look-ing for a rain-coat not too short, not too long, and not too ex-pen-sive, un-der fif-ty dol-lars. Here is one. Try it on.

Verses

Hector: Miss, I'm looking for a raincoat –
           not too short, not too long,
           and not too expensive, under fifty dollars.
  Clerk: Here is one. Try it on.

Hector: How much is this coat I'm wearing?
  Clerk: Forty–nine ninety–nine.
Hector: How much is the raincoat in the center window?
  Clerk: Eighty–nine ninety–nine.

Tune In To English

Hector: Now I'm looking for a sweater
made of wool, and dark green.
How much is the sweater in the center window?

Clerk: It's on sale for eighteen.

Hector: Well, I'd like to buy this raincoat
and that green sweater too.
Heavens! Where's my wallet? It was in my pocket.
Just my luck! Now I'm stuck.

Hector: Now I'm looking for my wallet.
It was small and dark brown.
I can't find my wallet. It was in my pocket.
Oh, good grief! Who's the thief?

Balloons

Complete the balloons. Refer to the song if you need help.

Match

Draw lines from the words to the objects.

pants

shirt

dress

wallet

shoes

umbrella

coat

sweater

socks

gloves

hat

tie

skirt

blouse

Multiple Choice

Broom goes into a store to buy something because he's cold. Study the pictures; then check the box next to the correct answer for each question.

1. What does Broom want to buy?
- ☐ a. A had
- ☐ b. A coat
- ☐ c. A scarf

2. What kind does Broom want?
- ☐ a. A long one
- ☐ b. A short one
- ☐ c. Any kind

3. What's he asking the saleswoman?
- ☐ a. How much is that?
- ☐ b. What's that?
- ☐ c. What's it made of?

4. What's the saleswoman saying?
- ☐ a. It's on sale.
- ☐ b. It's eight dollars.
- ☐ c. It's too expensive.

5. What's Broom saying?
- ☐ a. I'll take it.
- ☐ b. It's too expensive.
- ☐ c. Where's my wallet?

6. Did Broom buy the scarf?
- ☐ a. No, he didn't.
- ☐ b. Yes, he did.
- ☐ c. He lost his wallet.

13 What Would You Like To Eat?

Jean Wright has just finished playing a two–hour tennis match. Now she's at a restaurant. She's ordering a full meal, the special of the day. It includes steak cooked to taste, potatoes any style, salad, cheese, a choice of vegetables, and a choice of dessert. Jean is very hungry. Let's find out what she's ordering.

**Tune: Mexican Hat Dance
(Jarabe Tapatio)
Traditional Mexican song**

Hel - lo, please have a seat. What would you like to eat? I think I'll have a steak and then, for des - sert, some cake. Would you like it on a bun? Me - di - um? Rare? Per - haps well done? With some string beans or some peas? Po - ta - toes? Some sal - ad? Some cheese?

♪ Tune In To English

Verses

Waiter: Hello, please have a seat.
What would you like to eat?

Jean: I think I'll have a steak
and then, for dessert, some cake.

Waiter: Would you like it on a bun?
Medium? Rare? Perhaps well–done?
With some string beans or some peas?
Potatoes? Some salad? Some cheese?

Jean: I'd like my steak well–done,
served on a toasted bun.
I'd like some ketchup too.
Waiter: I'll fix it just right for you.

Jean: With a baked potato, please,
lots of string beans, lots of cheese,
and a salad would be nice,
and bring me some water with ice.

Balloons

What is the man saying to the waiter? Create your own cartoon. Use the clues to make sentences; then write them in the balloons.

She'd like/well–done/bun.

She'd like/some cake/dessert.

Grammarhyme

Complete each sentence of the rhyme with one of the words on the right. If you need help, refer back to the song on page 54.

Example:

Waiter:	Hello, Mrs. Fleet.	drink
	What would you like to___eat___?	eat
Mrs. Fleet:	Waiter, bring me please	cheese
	a sandwich with lettuce and _____.	tomatoes
Waiter:	Hello, Mr. Wink,	eat
	What would you like to _____?	drink
Mr. Wink:	Waiter, please bring me	coffee
	a cup of hot _____.	chocolate
Waiter:	Hello, Miss McNeet.	seat
	Come in and have a _____.	tea
	Would you like a steak?	toast
Miss McNeet:	Not today. Just coffee and _____.	cake

Balloons

Use the menu on the next page to complete the balloons.

LUNCH MENU

Today's Special   14.95

Steak with any style of potato and choice of vegetable (string beans or peas)
Includes salad, cheese, dessert, and coffee or tea

Soups

Soup of the day	1.95	Hamburger	4.95
Vegetable Soup	2.25	Cheeseburger with	
Onion Soup	2.25	lettuce and tomato	5.95
		Steak Sandwich with	
		French Fries	7.95

Salads   Desserts

Tossed salad	1.95	Ice cream	
Egg salad	4.95	small	1.45
Tuna salad	4.95	large	1.95
Chicken salad	5.95	Apple pie	2.95
		Cherry pie	2.95

Beverages

Coffee	.95
Tea	1.45
Milk	1.25
Soda	1.45

14 I'm Leaving for Peking

Joe Ling comes from San Francisco, California. His grandparents came to California from China many years ago. Joe has always wanted to visit China. Now he finally has a chance to take a trip there. He's talking to a travel agent right now about plane reservations.

Tune: Tom Dooley
Traditional American cowboy song

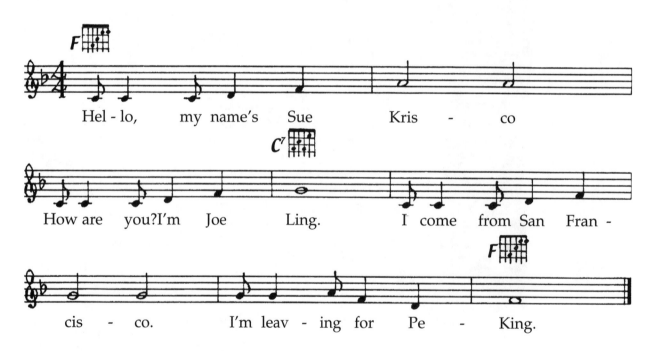

Hel - lo, my name's Sue Kris - co
How are you? I'm Joe Ling. I come from San Fran -
cis - co. I'm leav - ing for Pe - King.

Verses

Sue: Hello, my name's Sue Krisco.
Joe: How are you? I'm Joe Ling.
  I come from San Francisco.
  I'm leaving for Peking.

Sue: When are you going to go there?
Joe: Some time in March this year.
Sue: You'll need a reservation.
  I'll make it for you here.

Sue: What are you going to do there?
Joe: I'm going to learn Chinese.
   I know some words already –
   "Thank you," "hello," and "please."

Joe: Thanks for your help, Miss Krisco.
Sue: My pleasure, Mr. Ling.
   I hope you'll like your stay there.
   I hope you'll like Peking.

Answer the Questions

Answer the following questions based on the song.

1. Where does Joe Ling come from?

_____.

2. Where is he going?

_____.

3. When is he leaving?

_____.

4. What will he do there?

_____.

5. What will Sue Krisco do for him?

_____.

Jumbles

This young lady is going to France. She stops in to see a travel agent who discusses the trip with her. Unscramble the missing words to find out who she is, and when and why she's going to France.

Hello, my name's _____ Bassey.
                    (obb)

How are you? I'm _____ Day.
                   (aojn)

I come from Cincinnati.

I'm leaving for Marseilles.

When are you going to go there?

_____ in _____ this year.
    (lyare)   (neuj)

You'll need a reservation.

I'll make it for you here.

Where are you going to _____ _____?
            (tasy)   (onja)

I'll stay with my _____ _____.
         (nfider)   (rbat)

I've taken out a student _____.
              (olan)

I'm going to _____ _____.
      (dusyt)   (rta)

Balloons

Bill Blue comes from the planet Mars. He's planning a trip to the Earth. Complete the balloons using the hints below. Refer to the song if you need help.

Hints

1. Bill Blue   2. June this year   4. English

15 *Where's My Key?*

Bill is very afraid of being late for work. Sometimes he gets up late and then has to rush around to get ready in time. This makes him very nervous. Just before he leaves, he checks to see if he has everything. There's always something that he can't find, and he panics. This morning he can't find the key to the house. He wants his wife Janet to help him find it.

Tune: Jingle Bells

Where's my key? Where's my key? Have you seen my key?

I can't seem to find my key. Have you seen my key?

Where's my key? Where's my key? Have you seen my key?

I can't seem to find my key. Have you seen my key?

It's not by the door. It's not on the chair.

It's not on the floor. It's got to be some-where.

Tune In To English

It's not on the hook. It's not a - ny - where.

Can't you see I've looked and looked. I've looked just ev - ery - where.

Verses

Bill: Where's my key?
Where's my key?
Have you seen my key?
I can't seem to find my key.
Have you seen my key?

Where's my key?
Where's my key?
Have you seen my key?
I can't seem to find my key.
Have you seen my key?

It's not by the door.
It's not on the chair.
It's not on the floor.
It's got to be somewhere.

It's not on the hook.
It's not anywhere.
Can't you see, I've looked and looked.
I've looked just everywhere.

Janet: Come and look.
Come and look.
I've just found your key.
It's right on your key ring dear.
Where else would it be?
Come and look.

Come and look.
I've just found your key.
It's right on your key ring dear.
Where else would it be?

Jumbles

Michael tells Rhoda that he can't find his hat. If you unscramble the missing words, you'll find out where he looked for his hat and where it finally turned up.

Where's my hat? Where's my hat?
Have you seen my hat?
I can't seem to find my hat.
Have you seen my hat?
It's not on the _____.
        (cuhoc)
It's not in this _____.
        (moro)
Did you _____ it out?
        (ohtwr)
I've got to find it _____.
        (onos)
It's not in the _____.
        (lahl)

It's not on the _____.
        (krca)
There's no _____ of it at all.
        (ctrae)
I want to get it _____.
        (akcb)

Oh, my dear. Oh, my dear.
I've just _____ your hat.
        (nufdo)
It's right on your _____, my dear.
        (ahde)
You're _____ as a bat.
        (nilbd)

Search

The objects listed below are hidden in the picture. Can you find them? When you do, write a sentence describing where each one is located.

key   The key is _____.

hat   The hat is _____.

glove   The glove is _____.

scarf   The scarf is _____.

shoe   The shoe is _____.

Balloons

What are they looking for? Complete the balloons on the left and write the answers in the balloons on the right.

Have _____

_____ _____
        shoes?

_____

_____ hat?

16 Small Talk

At big parties you usually talk to a lot of different people. Sometimes you don't have much to say to a person, but you have to make "small talk"—superficial conversation filled with hellos and good–byes, questions about the family, comments on the weather, and sometimes promises about getting together soon. Here's a conversation between Mrs. Flynn and Mr. Blue, two business colleagues who run into each other at a party.

Tune: Oh Christmzas Tree (Oh Tannenbaum)
Traditional German song

Hi, Mrs._____ Flynn. Well, how've you been? What a sur-prise to see you. Hi, Mr._____ Blue. Well, how are you? It's real - ly great to see you. It's been so long since we last met. It's been at least a year. I bet. You're look - ing great, and I can't wait to hear what you've been up to.

Verses

Mr. Blue: Hi, Mrs. Flynn. Well, how've you been?
What a surprise to see you.

Mrs. Flynn: Hi, Mr. Blue. Well, how are you?
It's really great to see you.

Mr. Blue: It's been so long since we last met.
It's been at least a year, I bet.

Mrs. Flynn: You're looking great, and I can't wait
to hear what you've been up to.

Mr. Blue: Not much is new. But how about you?
You must have news to tell me.

Mrs. Flynn: I'm just the same. I can't complain,
except about my salary.

Mr. Blue: The weather's awful, isn't it?
It should be warmer, just a bit.

Mrs. Flynn: I think so too — I've had the flu,
and so has all my family.

Mr. Blue: There's my wife Eve. I've got to leave.
Let's hope for better weather.

Mrs. Flynn: Bye, Mr. Blue. Nice seeing you.
Next week let's get together.

Mr. Blue: Give me a call just anytime.
I'm in my office after nine.

Mrs. Flynn: I'll call you there. Bye–bye. Take care.
I'd love to get together.

Grammarhyme

Complete each sentence of the rhyme with one of the words on the right. Write the words in the blanks.

Example:

Hi, Mr. Blue.   are you

Well, how _____are you_____?   you been

Hi, Carolyn.   are you

How _____?   have you been

Oh, Annabell,   great

you're looking _____.   well

Well, Mrs. Hutch.   so much

Thanks _____.   a lot

My dear Mr. Chen,   today

nice seeing you _____.   again

There's my friend Steve.   go

I've got to _____.   leave

Goodnight, June.   soon

Let's get together _____.   later

Match

Draw lines to match the question in the first column with the right answer in the second column.

1. What do you say when you meet an old friend at a party?

2. What do you say when you want to know what an old friend has been doing recently?

3. What do you say when you want to pay a friend a compliment?

4. What do you say when you run into someone you weren't expecting to see?

5. What do you say when you're leaving your friend?

6. What do you say when you want to see your friend again soon?

a. What a surprise to see you.

b. I'd love to get together.

c. Bye–bye. Take care.

d. It's really great to see you.

e. I can't wait to hear what you've been up to.

f. You're looking great.

Balloons

Check the box next to the appropriate answer for each question in the balloons.

- ❑ a. The weather's awful.
- ❑ b. Fine. And you?
- ❑ c. I have to leave.
- ❑ d. It's great to see you.

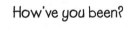

How've you been?

- ❑ a. It's been about a year.
- ❑ b. I'll call you.
- ❑ c. Let's get together.
- ❑ d. What a surprise to see you.

How long has it been since we last met?

17 Do You Know How This Works?

That racket you are hearing is coming from a nearby telephone booth. It is good old Harry Helpless. He's on business in London, and he is trying to make a telephone call to his office in Boston. Obviously, he has a problem. Let's listen as he asks two innocent bystanders for help.

Tune: LingoRap

Verses

(He asks a man.)

Harry Helpless: Do you know? Do you know? Do you know how this works?
Do you know? Do you know? Do you know how this works?

Man: I don't know. I don't know. I'm sorry, I don't know.
I don't know. I don't know. I'm sorry, I don't know.

Chorus: Do you know how this works?
Do you know how this works?

(He asks a young woman)

Harry Helpless: Do you know? Do you know? Do you know how this works?
Do you know? Do you know? Do you know how this works?

Young woman: First you do this, (inserts money)
and then you do that! (dials number)

Harry Helpless: First I do this, and than I do that?

Chorus: Do you know how this works? Do you know how this works?

Harry Helpless: Can you please, can you please, show it to me one more time?
Can you please, can you please, show it to me one more time?

Young woman: First you do this, (inserts money)
and then you do that! (dials number)

Harry Helpless: First I do this, (inserts money)
and than I do that?! (dials number)

Young woman: Goodness gracious!!!

Harry Helpless: Thank you for your help.

Young woman: No problem. My pleasure!

Match
Part A
Draw lines from column A to to the words in Column B that complete the sentences.

COLUMN A	COLUMN B

Example:

Do you know	do this.
I'm sorry,	show it to me once more time.
First you	I don't know.
and then you	how this works?
Can you please	your help.
Thank you	problem.
No,	do that.

Part B
How else can you say it? Draw a line from Column A to the sentence in Column B that is another way to say it.

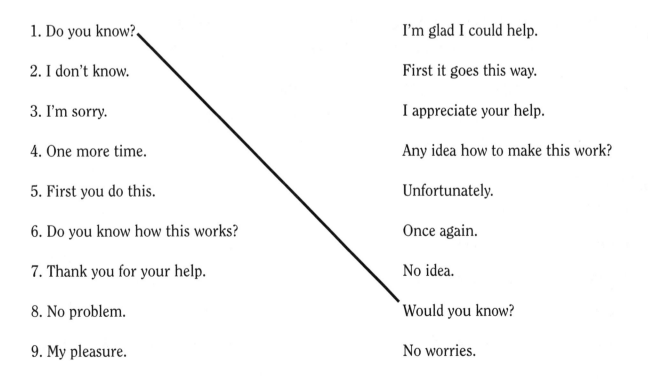

1. Do you know?	I'm glad I could help.
2. I don't know.	First it goes this way.
3. I'm sorry.	I appreciate your help.
4. One more time.	Any idea how to make this work?
5. First you do this.	Unfortunately.
6. Do you know how this works?	Once again.
7. Thank you for your help.	No idea.
8. No problem.	Would you know?
9. My pleasure.	No worries.

Puzzle

Can you find the words to the song in the maze below?

Harry Helpless: CANXWEX**DO**XXXXX**YOU**XXXXSEEXFINDX**KNOW**XXX
WHENXXHOWXXXWHYXXXTHEXXHISXTHISWORKS

Man: WEXEXXIXCANDON'TSEEXKNOWXIXXDON'TXKNOW
HEXSHEXI'MXXSORRYXIJUSTXXDON'TXCKNOWXXXX

Harry Helpless: EXCUSEMEBUTDOXXYOUPERHAPSXXXKNOWXXWE
DOESDOHEYOUYXCKNOWWHENHOWTHISWORKS

Young woman: LOOKFIRSTYOUMUSTDOBTHISBUTANDXTHENHE
WEXYOUXXDOXITEXACTLYTTHATXNOWXWATCHMEXC

Harry Helpless: OHXIXSEEXFIRSTXXTHEXIXMUSTXDOXXTHISXXANDX
ANDXXXTHENXAFTERWARDSXXXIMUSTXXDOXTHATX
COULDXWOULDXCANXXYOUXXNOWXPLEASEXXXCCC
GIVEXITXSHOWXITXXTOXXXMEXONEMOREXTIMEXXC

Youngwomen: NOWXLOOKXXMANFIRSTXXYOUXMUSTXDOXXTHISXX
NOWANDXAFTERWARDSTHENXXYOUCANDOXTHISXCC

Harry Helpless: OIXREALLYXTHANKXAPPRECIATEYOURXASSISTANCEX
VERYXMUCHFORXHISXHERXXYOURXXHELPXCVVCCC

Young women: OTHISXISQUITEXXALRIGHTXNOTHINGXPROBLEMTHIS
HISHEROOURMYXTIMEPLEASUREXANYXTIMEXXBYEX

Questions

Which answers are possible?

1. Do you know how this works? _____   a. My pleasure.

2. Can you show it to me one more time. _____   b. Sorry, I don't know.

3. Can you show it to me once again? _____   c. Not right now.

4. Thank you for your help! _____   d. First you do this, then you do that.

Example: 1. <u>b,d</u>

18 You're Drinking My Strawberry Shake

Laura Levine is sitting at a crowded lunch counter in a coffee shop in Chicago. Next to her there's an elegant young man named Lloyd Littlepage. Laura has never seen him before, but she's about to have a long conversation with him. Let's find out what they're saying to each other.

Tune: My Bonnie Lies Over The Ocean
American folk song

Ex - cuse me, I'm sor - ry to tell you, _____ but you took my drink by mis - take. _____ Ex - cuse me, I'm sor - ry to tell you, _____ you're drink-ing my straw- ber - ry shake. _____ I'm not. You are. Don't get up - set. ___ Don't raise your voice. I'm not. You are. Please don't raise your voice to me. _____

Verses

Lloyd: Excuse me, I'm sorry to tell you
but you took my drink by mistake
Excuse me, I'm sorry to tell you
you're drinking my strawberry shake.

Laura: I'm not.

Lloyd: You are.

Laura: Don't get upset. Don't raise your voice.

Lloyd: I'm not.

Laura: You are.

Lloyd: Please don't raise your voice to me.

Laura: And what makes you think it's
your milkshake?
I think you must be color blind
And what makes you think it's
your milkshake?
I think that you're out of your mind.

Lloyd: I'm not.

Laura: You are.

Lloyd: Let's let the manager say who's right.

Laura: All right.

Lloyd: All right.

Laura: Let's have him settle the fight.

Balloons

What are they saying? Use the clues under the pictures to make sentences; then write them in the balloons.

took/tray/mistake.

raise/voice/me.

Jumbles

Unscramble the missing words and write them in the blank spaces.

Spiderwoman: Excuse me, I'm sorry to _____ you   (lelt)

but you took my _____ by mistake.   (lapet)

Excuse me, I'm sorry to tell you,

you're _____ my strawberry _____.   (teanig)
(ekac)

King Strong: I'm _____.   (ton)

Spiderwoman: You _____.   (rea)

King Strong: Don't get _____. Don't raise your voice.   (uteps)

Spiderwoman: Who _____?   (si)

King Strong: You _____.   (rea)

Spiderwoman: _____ don't raise your _____ to me.   (sleeap)
(ievco)

Puzzle

Did Miss Levine drink Mr. Littlepage's milkshake by mistake? Who's right, and who's wrong? The manager came and tasted the drink. What did he find out? Solve the puzzle to find out what the drink was. Write your answer below.

1. Dear lady, I'm c to tell you

2. but you took my _____ by mistake.

3. Dear _____, I'm sorry to tell you, you're drinking my strawberry shake.

4. I'm _____.

5. Don't _____ upset.

6. Don't raise your voice to _____.

7. –J–

8. _____ must be color blind.

9. You must be out of your _____.

10. Don't raise your _____.

11. I'm calling _____ manager now.

The drink was _____.

(answer to puzzle)

19 Surprise Party

Surprise birthday parties can be a lot of fun. Today is Larry's birthday. His friends wanted to surprise him with a party. So they sneaked into his apartment with a birthday cake and waited for him to come home. Unfortunately, Larry decided to come home late, and the party began before he got there. Here's what he found when he got home.

Tune: Ode To Joy
German song by Ludwig van Beethoven

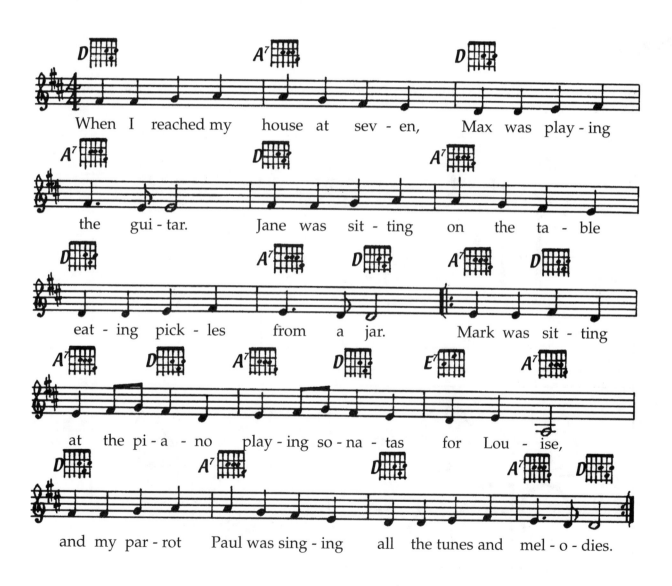

When I reached my house at sev - en, Max was play - ing
the gui - tar. Jane was sit - ting on the ta - ble
eat - ing pick - les from a jar. Mark was sit - ting
at the pi - a - no play - ing so - na - tas for Lou - ise,
and my par - rot Paul was sing - ing all the tunes and mel - o - dies.

Verses

When I reached my house at seven,
Max was playing the guitar.
Jane was sitting on the table
eating pickles from a jar.

Mark was sitting at the piano
playing sonatas for Louise,
and my parrot Paul was singing
all the tunes and melodies.

Bob was sleeping under the table;
he couldn't even stay awake.
And my dog was in the kitchen
eating up the birthday cake.

Puzzles

Max plays the guitar and two other instruments. Solve the picture puzzles to rind out what other instruments he plays.

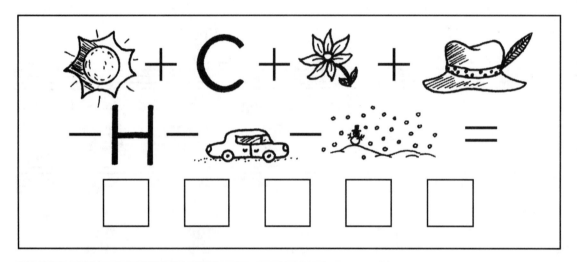

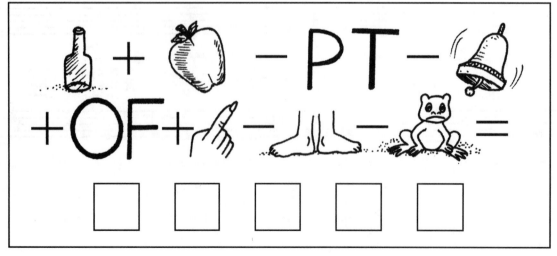

Fill-Ins

On the following day Liz called her friend Beverly and told her about the surprise party for Larry. Fill in the blanks with the correct word from the right to find out what Liz said.

When Larry reached _____ house at seven

my
his

Max was _____ his guitar.

playing
eating

Jane was _____ on the table

sleeping
sitting

eating pickles from a _____.

plate
jar

Mark was sitting at the _____

piano
table

playing _____ for Louise.

folk songs
sonatas

And _____ parrot Paul was singing

his
your

all the tunes and _____.

songs
melodies

Bob _____ the table;

was sleeping under
was standing under

he couldn't even _____.

stay awake
fall asleep

And _____ dog was in the kitchen

our
his

eating up the _____.

well–done steak
birthday cake

Complete

Everyone in the Holmes family was doing something different when Mrs. Holmes came home. Choose from the list on the right and complete the sentences with the correct form of the verb.

Her husband was _____.   dance

The baby was _____.   do a headstand

Her son Billy was _____.   play the guitar

Grandma Holmes was _____.   sleep

Her daughter Lily was _____.   paint the kitchen

Fred the dog was _____.   read a book

20 I Miss You So My Dear

Keiko is from Osaka and George is from Los Angeles. They met in London last year. They fell in love. Now Keiko is back in Japan and George is back in the United States. They miss each other very much. They plan to meet in London again next year. Until then, they can only write letters or talk on the telephone. The other day George decided to call Keiko in Osaka to give her a surprise. He dialed her number and started singing this song.

Tune: Down By The Riverside
American Negro spiritual

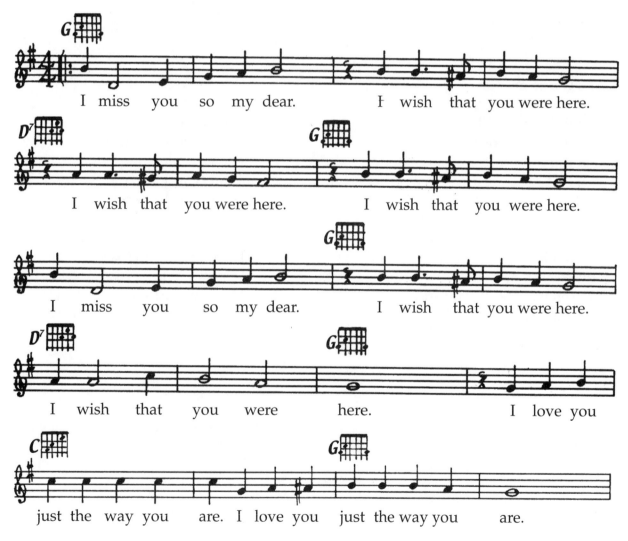

CHAPTER 20: I MISS YOU SO MY DEAR

Cra - zy, or blue, or mad. I love you just the way you are. I love you just the way you are. Cra - zy, or blue, or mad._____

Verses

I miss you so my dear.
I wish that you were here.
I wish that you were here.
I wish that you were here.
I miss you so my dear.
I wish that you were here.
I wish that you were here.

I love you just the way you are.
I love you just the way you are.
Crazy, or blue, or mad.
I love you just the way you are.
I love you just the way you are.
Crazy, or blue, or mad.

I hope you love me too,
as much as I love you,
as much as I love you,
as much as I love you.
I hope you love me too,
as much as I love you,
as much as I love you.

I love you just the way you are.
I love you just the way you are.
Crazy, or blue, or mad.
I love you just the way you are.
I love you just the way you are.
Crazy, or blue, or mad.

When George finished his song there was a long silence. To find out why, turn to page 83.

TUNE IN TO ENGLISH

Puzzles

George wanted to surprise his friend Keiko, but in the end George was surprised. To find out why, solve puzzles A and B.

Puzzle A

Fill in the puzzle boxes with the words missing from the clues. Number 1 down is the answer.

1. I _____ you so my dear.

2. I miss you _____ my dear.

3. I love you _____ the way you are.

4. I wish _____ you were here.

5. I love you just the way you _____.

6. I wish that you were _____.

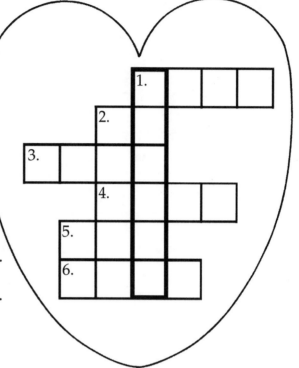

Puzzle B

Add the letter T to the name of a big animal living in Africa and in India. Then subtract the letters that spell the name of a little animal that lives in a sand hill. Add the letters that spell the number 1 and you have the answer.

George was surprised because Keiko's _____ was on the _____.

 answer to puzzle A   answer to puzzle B

Complete

Keiko was not at home to receive George's telephone call. But Keiko's mother answered him. To find out what she said to George, complete each sentence with the correct form of the verb on the right.

She _____ you my dear. (to miss)

She _____ you were here. (to wish)

She _____ you were here. (to wish)

She _____ you were here. (to wish)

She _____ you my dear. (to miss)

She _____ you were here. (to wish)

She _____ you just the way you are. (to love)

She _____ you just the way you are. (to love)

Crazy, or blue, or mad.

She _____ you just the way you are. (to love)

She _____ you just the way you are. (to love)

Crazy, or blue, or mad.

She _____ you love her too, (to hope)

as much as she loves you,

as much as she loves you,

as much as she loves you.

She _____ you love her too, (to hope)

as much as she loves you.

She _____ you love her too. (to hope)

Check your answers in the answer key. Then sing your new song.

21 *Sorry You Had To Wait*

Mrs. Montesquieu is waiting on a street corner for her husband. She has been waiting since she left work at five. He was supposed to drive to town and pick her up after work so that they could go out to dinner. But he's a little late and he's apologizing to her.

Tune: Santa Lucia
Italian folk song

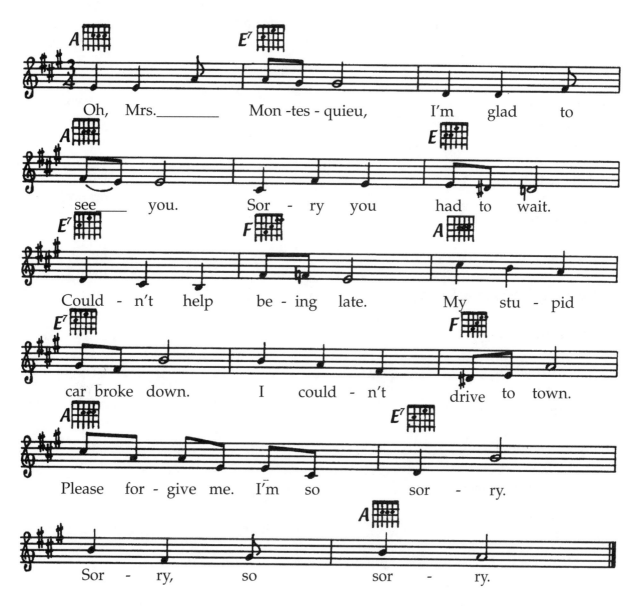

Oh, Mrs._____ Mon-tes-quieu, I'm glad to see_____ you. Sor-ry you had to wait. Could-n't help be-ing late. My stu-pid car broke down. I could-n't drive to town. Please for-give me. I'm so sor-ry. Sor-ry, so sor-ry.

Verses

Mr. M:
Oh, Mrs. Montesquieu,
I'm glad to see you.
Sorry you had to wait.
Couldn't help being late.
My stupid car broke down.
I couldn't drive to town.
Please forgive me. I'm so sorry.
Sorry, so sorry.

Mrs. M:
Dear Mr. Montesquieu,
I'm glad to see you too.
I didn't mind the wait.
You're just three hours late.
It's only ten below,
and I don't mind the snow.
You don't have to say you're sorry,
sorry, so sorry.

Grammarhyme

Complete the sentences of the rhyme with the correct words from the right.

Oh, my Penny Sue,

I'm glad to see _____.

everyone
you

Sorry you had to wait.

Couldn't help being _____.

late
on time

My bicycle broke down.

I had to walk to _____.

home
town

Please forgive me. I'm so sorry.

Oh, my Willy dear,

I'm glad that you're _____.

back
here

I didn't mind the wait.

You're just an hour _____.

late
early

You don't have to say you're sorry.

Balloons

Roy Rabbit is going to see a play with his friend Ted Turtle. They were supposed to meet at six o'clock. It's now seven thirty and Ted hasn't arrived yet. Complete the balloons. You can refer to the song if you need help.

Balloons

Fill in each of the balloons with what you think the characters are saying.

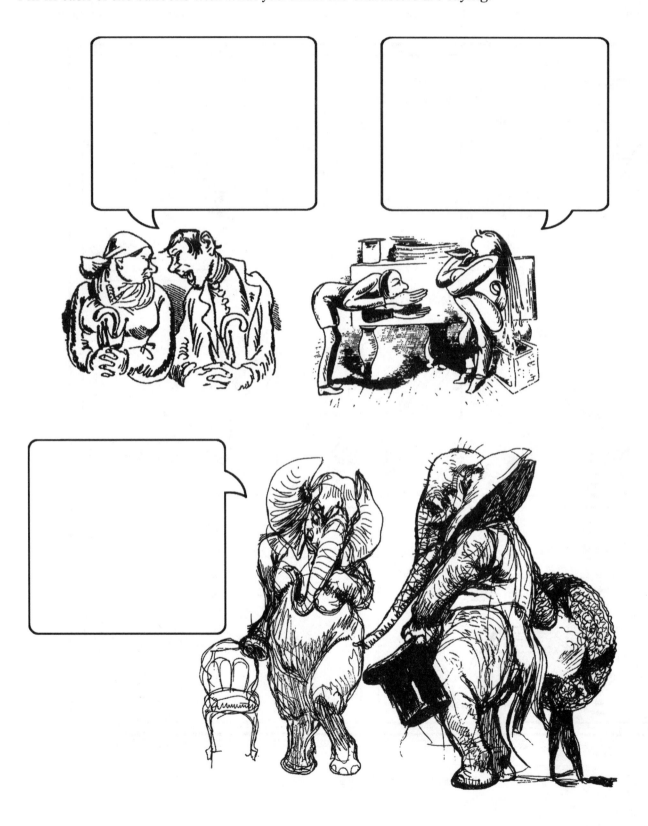

22 I Just Want My Money Back

Ana Serrano runs a store in a small town in the state of Nevada. She sells all kinds of things: food, clothes, dishes, tools, appliances, and even plants. Today Ana has a few unhappy customers. They want to return merchandise that they bought.

Tune: The Blue Danube
    Austrian Waltz by Johann Strauss

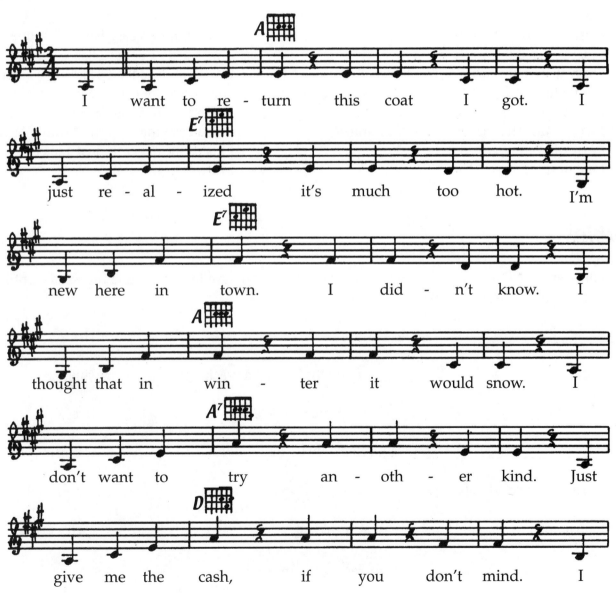

I want to re - turn this coat I got. I just re - al - ized it's much too hot. I'm new here in town. I did - n't know. I thought that in win - ter it would snow. I don't want to try an - oth - er kind. Just give me the cash, if you don't mind. I

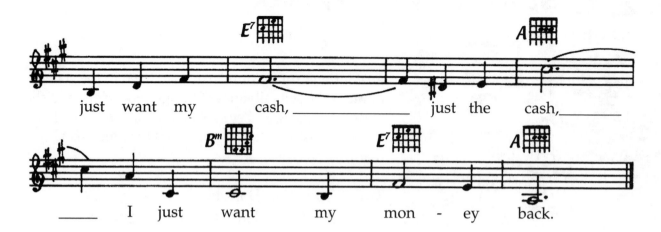

just want my cash, _____ just the cash, _____

____ I just want my mon - ey back.

Verses

Jean McGee:
I want to return this coat I got.
I just realized it's much too hot.
I'm new here in town. I didn't know.
I thought that in winter it would snow.
I don't want to try another kind.
Just give me the cash, if you don't mind.
I just want my cash, just the cash.
I just want my money back.

Sam Sweet:
Miss, could I please have my money back?
This teacup I bought has got a crack.
I paid you by check. Here's my receipt,
and here's my I.D., my name's Sam Sweet.
The price on it was $5.59.
If you gave me cash, that would be fine.
I just want my cash, just the cash.
I just want my money back.

Jumbles

Here's a different version of the song. Before you can sing it you have to unscramble the words on the right and write them in the proper blanks to complete the sentences.

_____, could I please get my money back.   ris

This white _____ I bought has got a crack.   lapet

I paid you by _____. Here's my receipt.   hkcek

My _____'s right here. My name's Joe Reed.   passortp

The price on it was $12.98.

If you give me _____ that would be _____.   asch   grtea

I _____ want my cash, just the cash.   stuj

I just want my _____ back.   nemyo

Complete

Study the pictures. Then complete the sentences.

1. I want to return this _____.

a

   It's _____. Just look at that.

b

   Can I have a _____?

c

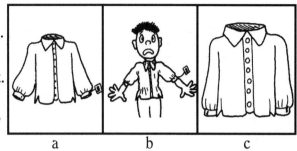

a   b   c

2. I want to return this _____.

a

   The _____.

b

   I'd like to get _____.

c

a   b   c

3. _____.

a

   The _____.

b

   Can I have _____.

c

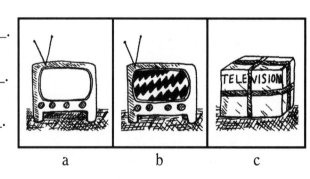

a   b   c

4. _____.

a

   It _____.

b

   Could I please get _____?

c

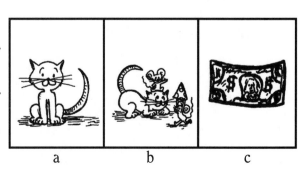

a   b   c

Chapter 22: I Just Wanted My Money Back

Write

Mrs. Armstrong is talking to a salesman about a plate she bought. Go over the song again. Then write what she's saying on the lines next to each picture.

1._____

_____ .

2._____

_____ .

3._____

_____ .

Review

Detective

Can you detect what's wrong with each of these song lines? Write the correct lines in the spaces provided. Refer to the songs if you need help.

1. Miss, I'm looking for a string bean—not too short, not too long.

_____

_____

2. Hello, please have a book. What would you like to eat?

_____

_____

3. I come from San Francisco. I'm flying to the bathroom.

_____

_____

4. I can't seem to find my head. Have you seen my head?

_____

_____

5. It's been so long since we last slept. It's been at least ten feet, I bet.

_____

_____

6. Excuse me, I'm sorry to tell you but you took my scarf in your mouth.

_____

_____

7. When I reached my knee at seven, Max was playing Santa Claus.

_____

_____

8. I love you so my dear. I wish that you weren't here.

_____

_____

9. Sorry you had to fall. Couldn't help being tall.

_____

_____

10. Miss, could I please have my milkshake back? This coat that I bought has got a crack.

_____

_____

Jumbles

If you rearrange the words in each line, you'll have a sentence from one of your songs. Write the correct sentence and the name of the tune it's from.

1. is much center the in how the sweater window

_____

_____

2. like you your would well steak done

_____

_____

3. to there do what going you are

_____

_____

4. and looked see you can't I've looked

_____

_____

5. really it's see to great you

_____

_____

6. let say let's who's manager the right

_____

_____

7. on jar Jane the sitting was table pickles a from eating

_____

_____

8. the just you love I are way you

_____

_____

9. have don't you're you to sorry say

_____

_____

10. would gave you if be gave fine cash me that

_____

_____

Answer Key

1: I'm Glad To Meet You

Jumbles *(page 2)*

This is Mario.
He's from <u>Italy</u>.
He speaks <u>Italian</u>.

This is Monique.
She's from <u>France</u>.
She speaks <u>French</u>.

This is Uwe and this is Ulla.
They're from <u>Germany</u>.
They speak <u>German</u>.

This is Katsura.
She's from <u>Japan</u>.
She speaks <u>Japanese</u>.

This is Geraldo.
He's from <u>Brazil</u>.
He speaks <u>Portuguese</u>.

This is Carlos and this is Maria.
They're from <u>Mexico</u>.
They speak <u>Spanish</u>.

Grammarhyme *(page 4)*

I'm from London. My name's Tom Thumb.
What's your name and <u>where're you from</u>?

Are you Mr. Jerry Spot?
<u>No, I'm not</u>.

This is Mrs. Lucy Bell.
She speaks English <u>very well</u>.

How do you do?
I'm glad <u>to meet you</u>.

This is Mrs. Linda Austin.
Mrs. Austin is from <u>Boston</u>.

This is Mr. Freddy Freeze.
He speaks English and <u>Japanese</u>.

Balloons *(page 5)*

1. Do you speak <u>English</u>?

2. Yes, but <u>just</u> a little <u>bit</u>.

3. <u>Are</u> you from <u>Moscow</u>?

4. No, <u>I'm</u> not. I'm from <u>Peru</u>.

5. My name is <u>Sylvia</u>.

6. What's your <u>name</u> and where're <u>you from</u>?

7. My name is <u>Elvis</u>. I'm from <u>Nashville, Tennessee</u>.

8. I'm <u>glad</u> to meet you. I'm so <u>glad</u> to <u>meet</u> you <u>too</u>.

2: There's A Little Grocery Store Right Across The Street

Complete *(page 7)*

Where can I get some <u>toothpaste</u>, Pete?
There's a <u>pharmacy</u> across the street.

Where can I get some <u>flowers</u>. Pete?
There's a <u>florist (shop)</u> across the street.

I need some <u>cheese</u>, Pete.
There's a <u>grocery (store)</u> across the street.

I need some <u>lamb chops</u>. Pete.
There's a butcher (shop) across the street.

Where can I get some bread, Pete?
There's a <u>bakery (pastry shop)</u> across the street.

Where can I get some <u>money</u>, Pete?
There's a <u>bank</u> across the street.

Match *(page 8)*

book — bookstore

fruit — grocery store

milk — grocery store

plant — florist shop

money — bank

toothbrush — pharmacy

lamb chop — butcher shop

flowers — florist shop

bread — bakery

aspirin — pharmacy

Puzzles *(page 9)*

TEA + SKIRT + EE - TREE - I = A S K T E = $\boxed{S}$ $\boxed{T}$ $\boxed{E}$ $\boxed{A}$ $\boxed{K}$

BED + CAR - C = B E D A R = $\boxed{B}$ $\boxed{R}$ $\boxed{E}$ $\boxed{A}$ $\boxed{D}$

3: How Much Is It?

Grammarhyme *(page 11)*

Mrs. Bissett,
<u>How much does it</u> cost?

Now I'm lost!
<u>How much does it</u> cost?

Ms. Hutch,
<u>How much does it</u> cost?

O'Neal, let's buy it.
<u>It's such a good deal.</u>

This is nice
<u>and a very good price.</u>

Ms. Ash, can you
<u>pay me in cash?</u>

How much is your fee?
<u>Eighty three.</u>

I want that door.
<u>How much does it sell for?</u>

Write a New Dialog *(page 12)*

Hello!
Hello. May I help you?
How much is this CD player?

This CD player here is forty five dollars.
Forty two dollars? That's more than I thought.
It's a very good price.
I don't want to spend that much.
How much can you spend?
All I have is thirty two dollars.
Alright, thirty two for you.
I will take it for thirty two.
Thank you. Good bye.
Good bye.

Match *(page 13)*

What do you say when you want to know the price?
<u>How much does it sell for?</u>

What do you say when something is too expensive?
<u>That's expensive.</u>

What do you say when something nice costs very little?
<u>That's a good deal.</u>

What do you say when you're on a low budget?
<u>That's more than I thought.</u>

How do you ask for a price of an item?
<u>How much is it?</u>

4: My Father Has a Sister

Puzzle *(page 15)*

Family Circle *(page 16)*

1.b	4.a
2.b	5.c
3.d	6.a

Balloons *(page 17)*

Picture 1: Sir, is that <u>your</u> car?
    No, it's not <u>my</u> car.

Picture 2: Maybe It's <u>her</u> car?

Picture 3: Miss, Is that <u>your</u> car?
    No, it's not <u>my</u> car.

Picture 4: Maybe It's <u>his</u> car.

Picture 5: Is that <u>your</u> car, sir?
    I don't drive.

Picture 6: But maybe it's <u>their</u> car?

Picture 7: Is that <u>your</u> car over there?

Picture 8: That's not <u>our</u> car.

Picture 9: I think it's <u>my</u> car.

5. First Turn Right at the Light

Grammarhyme *(page 19)*

Pardon, sir.
Please tell <u>her</u>
how to get to downtown London.

Her friends Sam and Sara Shore
live at South Street number <u>four</u>.

First turn right
at the <u>light</u>.

Pass the pool,
and pass the <u>school</u>

Pass the old wall,
pass the <u>town hall</u>

Pass the bench in front of the store,
and that is South Street number <u>four</u>.

Balloons *(page 20)*

1. Pardon me. Please <u>tell me</u> how to <u>get to</u> 4 East 12th Street.
The address you're <u>looking</u> for is close.

2. I'll just <u>follow</u> your <u>directions</u>.

3. Walk <u>one</u> block, then turn <u>right</u>. Walk <u>two</u> more <u>blocks</u>.

4. Turn <u>left</u>. That's 12th Street. Number <u>four</u> is the second house on the <u>right</u>.

5. Now I <u>know</u> where to <u>go</u>. <u>Thanks</u> so much.

6. You're quite <u>welcome</u>. Any <u>time</u>.

Giving Directions *(page 21)*

(Suggested answers.)

Walk three blocks. Pass the baker and the bookstore.

Pass the bank and turn left at the light.

Turn left again at the next corner and pass the park.

Turn right at the corner in front of the hotel.

Turn right again at the next corner and pass the toy store.

Walk two blocks and the school is on your left.

6. Merry Christmas

Word Hunt *(page 23)*

Balloons *(page 24)*

What is the woman saying to the waiter?
    a. Bring him a knife, please.

What is the woman saying to the clerk?
    c. Give her a stamp. please.

What is the girl saying to her father?
    b. Buy me a chair for my table.

Make A Wish *(page 21)*

The objects in the picture are a plane, a guitar, a horse, a sports car, and a sailboat.

7. Copycat

Fill-Ins *(page 27)*

(Possible answers.)

I like to <u>take a walk every day</u>.

I like to <u>read</u>.

I also like to <u>listen to music</u>.

I don't like to <u>sew</u>.

I don't like to <u>dance</u>.

I don't like to <u>sleep too much</u> either.

Answer the Questions *(page 28)*

Does Jenny like to take a bath every day?
<u>No, Jenny doesn't like to take a bath every day.</u>

Does Jenny like to study English every day?
<u>Yes, Jenny likes to study English every day.</u>

Does Jenny like to do a headstand every day?
<u>Yes, Jenny likes to do a headstand every day.</u>

Does Jenny like to take a shower every day?
<u>Yes, Jenny likes to take a shower every day.</u>

Does Jenny like to sleep till noon every day?
<u>Yes, Jenny likes to sleep till noon every day.</u>

Balloons *(page 28)*

1. b. He likes to watch TV every day.

2. a. Broom likes to drink milk every day.

3. c. Broom likes to dance every day.

4. b. Broom likes to run Lu the park every day.

5. c. He likes to take a shower every day.

8. I Feel Happy Today

Grammarhyme (page 31)

This Is Mr. Zappy.
He's feeling very <u>happy</u>.
It's been sunny all day.
He feels happy today.

This Is Miss Peekaboo.
She feels terribly <u>blue</u>.
She tells her cat Sue
that she doesn't know what <u>to do</u>.

This is Judy Spence.
At work she's nervous and <u>tense</u>.
Judy's boss, Jane Fence,
thinks it doesn't make much <u>sense</u>.

This is Mrs. Langry.
Today she feels quite <u>angry</u>.
She's had a bad day,
so stay out of her <u>way</u>.

Write (page 32)

(Suggested answers.)

1. I feel happy when the sun shines.

2. I feel blue when it rains.

3. I feel tense when I have to take a test.

4. I feel very happy when I'm at a party.

5. I feel angry when someone I'm supposed to meet is late.

Balloons (page 32)

(Suggested answers.)

Balloon 1: I feel angry today.

Balloon 2: I feel nervous and tense today.

Balloon 3: We feel happy today.

Balloon 4: I feel blue today.

9: In Front of My House There's a Tree

Draw (page 35)

What did you draw? A house.

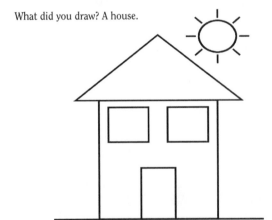

Balloons (page 36)

1. b

2. a

3. c

Fill–Ins (page 37)

1. under

2. on top of

3. in front of

4. next to

5. on

6. on

7. on top of

10: Wrong Number

Grammarhyme (page 40)

I'm calling from Rome.
Is Mrs. Yellow <u>home</u>?

Sorry, Mr. Fellow.
This is not Mrs. <u>Yellow</u>.

My name's Betty Lumber.
You have the wrong <u>number</u>.

I'd like to talk to Lynn.
She's not <u>in</u>.

Puzzles (page 40)

W + IRON – I + G = W R O N G = | W | R | O | N | G |

CAR – C + EAR – R = A R E A = | A | R | E | A |

COAT + H – HAT + DE = C O D E = | C | O | D | E |

Balloons (page 41)

(Suggested answers.)

1. Hello. My name's Fido. Can I speak to Rover, please?
   Oh, no. I think you've got the wrong number, my friend.

2. Am I speaking to my prince?
   You've dialed the wrong number.

3. Hello, hello. Can I speak to Mrs. Claus?
   I'm not Mrs. Claus. You have the wrong number.

11: Greetings From Italy

Grammarhyme *(page 43)*

My dear Susannah, how are you?
I'm having lots of <u>fun</u>.

Just yesterday I got sunstroke
from sleeping in the <u>sun</u>.

The weather here's been beautiful.
It's only rained all <u>week</u>.

My stomach doesn't like the food
and nothing here is <u>cheap</u>.

Oh, Susannah!
I hate the blue, blue <u>sea</u>.

I hope I'll see you all real soon.
Sincerely, your friend <u>Lee</u>.

Greetings *(page 45)*

(Suggested answers.)

Dear _____<u>Tom</u>_____,

How are you? I'm _____<u>fine</u>_____.

I need _____<u>more money</u>_____.

This place is _____<u>expensive</u>_____.

The weather is _____<u>wonderful</u>_____.

I think about you _____<u>often</u>_____.

I hope you are _____<u>well</u>_____.

Give my best to _____<u>our friends</u>_____.

_____<u>Best wishes</u>_____,

_____<u>Your Name</u>_____

Mr. Tom Long
2018 Albany Street
Yorkville, NY 10802

Jumbles *(page 44)*

Our dearest <u>Freddy</u>, how are you?
We're <u>fine</u>, as you can see.
Right now we're spending <u>three</u> nice weeks
in northern <u>Germany</u>.

Oh, dear <u>Freddy</u>!
Regards from <u>Germany</u>.
Say <u>hello</u> to all our friends,
and to your <u>family</u>.

Although the weather's <u>very</u> cold
we go out <u>every</u> day.
We're meeting lots of <u>people</u> here.
Don't know how long we'll <u>stay</u>.

Oh, <u>dear</u> Freddy!
Regards from <u>Germany</u>.
Give our love to all our <u>friends</u>.
and to <u>your</u> family.

REVIEW

Detective *(page 46)*

1. Do you speak English? Yes, but just a little bit.

2. I need flowers, Pete. There's a little florist shop right across the street.

3. My father has a sister and her name's Patricia Grant.

4. First turn right at the light, walk two blocks, stop at the corner.

5. Bring her gloves for the cold. Bring her earrings made of gold.

6. Every time I take a shower, she takes a shower. Oh, she likes to do what I do every day.

7. I feel happy today. It's been sunny all day.

8. Around my house there's a lawn. On weekends I sit there till dawn.

9. I think that you've got the wrong number, my friend. You've dialed a garage in Montana.

10. I lost my wallet yesterday in front of the hotel. Please send me money right away.

Jumbles *(page 48)*

1. What's your name and where are you from? "I'm Glad To Meet You"

2. There's a little pharmacy right across the street. "There's A Little Grocery Store Right Across The Street"

3. Can you tell me who Chris Is? "My Father Has A Sister"

4. Please tell me how to get to Greenwich Village. "First Turn Right At The Light"

5. Bring me chocolate, candy canes, and nuts. "Merry Christmas"

6. Every time I sleep till noontime she sleeps till noontime. "Copycat"

7. I'm so mad at the whole world. "I Feel Happy Today"

8. Across the road there's a lake where I go swimming with Jake. "In Front Of My House"

9. My name's Joe Monroe and I'm calling from Indiana. "Wrong Number"

10. Say hello to everyone and lots of love from me. "Greetings From Italy"

12: I'm Looking for a Raincoat

Balloons *(page 51)*

1. Miss, I'm <u>looking</u> <u>for</u> a jacket.

2. Here's one. <u>Try</u> <u>it</u> on.

3. How <u>much</u> <u>is</u> <u>this</u> jacket?

4. It's <u>forty-nine ninety-nine</u>. (possible answer)

5. Well, I'd like <u>to</u> <u>buy</u> this jacket.

6. Oh, <u>good</u> <u>grief</u>! I can't <u>find</u> <u>my</u> <u>wallet</u>.

Multiple Choice *(page 53)*

1. c	4. b
2. a	5. a
3. a	6. b

Match *(page 52)*

pants
shirt
dress
wallet
shoes
umbrella
coat
sweater
socks
gloves
hat
tie
skirt
blouse

13: What Would You Like to Eat

Balloons *(page 55)*

1. She'd like a well-done steak served on a bun.

2. She'd like some cake for dessert.

Grammarhyme *(page 56)*

Mrs. Fleet: Waiter, bring me please
a sandwich with lettuce and <u>cheese</u>.

Waiter: Hello, Mr. Wink.
What would you like to <u>drink</u>?

Mr. Wink: Waiter, please bring me
a cup of hot <u>coffee</u>.

Waiter: Hello, Miss McNeet.
Come in and have a <u>seat</u>.

Would you like a steak?
Miss McNeet: Not today. Just coffee and <u>cake</u>.

Balloons *(page 56)*

(Suggested answers.)

1. <u>Hello</u>, please have a <u>seat</u>.
<u>Thank</u> you.

2. What <u>would</u> <u>you</u> like to eat?

3. I think I'll have <u>a cheeseburger without the lettuce and tomato</u>.

4. Anything to drink?
Yes, <u>a soda</u>, please.

5. And for dessert?
I'll have <u>a large ice cream</u>.

6. Is everything all right?
Yes, just fine, <u>thank you</u>.

14: I'm Leaving for Peking

Answer the Questions (page 59)

1. Joe Ling comes from San Francisco.

2. He's going to Peking.

3. He's leaving some time in March this year.

4. He's going to learn Chinese.

5. Sue Krisco will make a reservation for him.

Jumbles (page 60)

Hello, my name's <u>Bob</u> Bassey.

How are you? I'm <u>Joan</u> Day.

I come from Cincinnati.

I'm leaving for Marseilles.

When are you going to go there?

<u>Early</u> in <u>June</u> this year.

You'll need a reservation.

I'll make it for you here.

Where are you going to <u>stay</u>, <u>Joan</u>?

I'll stay with my <u>friend Bait</u>

I've taken out a student <u>loan</u>.

I'm going to <u>study art</u>.

Balloons (page 61)

1. Hello, <u>my</u> <u>name's</u> Jean Sharp.
How do you do? I'm <u>Bill</u> <u>Blue</u>. I <u>come</u> <u>from</u> the planet Mars. <u>I'm</u> <u>leaving</u> <u>for</u> the Earth.

2. When <u>are</u> <u>you</u> <u>going</u> <u>to</u> <u>go</u> <u>there</u>?
Some <u>time</u> <u>in</u> <u>June</u> <u>this</u> <u>year</u>.

3. You'll need <u>a</u> <u>reservation</u>. I'll make it <u>for</u> <u>you</u> <u>here</u>.

4. What are you <u>going</u> <u>to</u> <u>do</u> <u>there</u>?
I'm <u>going</u> <u>to</u> <u>learn</u> <u>English</u>.

5. Here <u>is</u> your ticket.
Thanks <u>for</u> <u>your</u> <u>help</u>, Miss Sharp.

6. My <u>pleasure</u>. I hope <u>you'll</u> <u>like</u> <u>the</u> <u>Earth</u>.

15: Where's My Key

Jumbles (page 63)

It's not on the <u>couch</u>.

It's not in this <u>room</u>.

Did you <u>throw</u> it out?

I've got to find it <u>soon</u>.

It's not in the <u>hall</u>.

It's not on the <u>rack</u>.

There's no <u>trace</u> of it at all.

I want to get it <u>back</u>.

Oh, my dear. Oh, my dear.

I've just <u>found</u> your hat.

It's right on your <u>head</u>, my dear.

You're <u>blind</u> as a bat.

Search (page 64)

The key is on top of the book.

The hat is on top of the table.

The glove is on the chair.

The scarf is on the window.

The shoe is under the TV.

Balloons (page 65)

1. Have you <u>seen my shoes</u>? <u>They're on your feet</u>.

2. <u>Where's</u> <u>my</u> hat? <u>It's on your head</u>.

16: Small Talk

Grammarhyme (page 68)

Hi, Carolyn.
How <u>have you been</u>?

Oh, Annabell,
you're looking <u>well</u>.

Well, Mrs. Hutch.
Thanks <u>so much</u>.

My dear Mr. Chen,
nice seeing you <u>again</u>.

There's my friend Steve.
I've got to <u>leave</u>.

Goodnight, June.
Let's get together <u>soon</u>.

Match (page 69)

1. d (or a)

2. e

3. f

4. a (or d)

5. c

6. b

Balloons (page 69)

First picture: b. Fine. And you?

Second picture: a. It's been about a year.

17: Do You Know How This Works

Match (page 71)

Part A

Do you know <u>how this works</u>?
I'm sorry, <u>I don't know</u>.
First you <u>do this</u>.
and then you <u>do that</u>.
Can you please <u>show it to me once more time</u>.
Thank you <u>for your help</u>.
No, <u>problem</u>.

Part B

1. Do you know? / <u>Would you know?</u>
2. I don't know. / <u>No idea.</u>
3. I'm sorry. / <u>Unfortunately.</u>
4. One more time. / <u>Once again.</u>
5. First you do this. / <u>First it goes this way.</u>
6. Do you know how this works? / <u>Any idea how to make this work?</u>
7. Thank you for your help. / <u>I appreciate your help.</u>
8. No problem. / <u>No worries.</u>
9. My pleasure. / <u>I'm glad I could help.</u>

Puzzle (page 72)

Harry Helpless: CANXWEX<u>DO</u>XXXXX<u>YOU</u>XXXXSEEXFINDX<u>KNOW</u>XX
WHENXX<u>HOW</u>XXXWHYXXXTHEXXHISX<u>THIS</u><u>WORKS</u>

Man: WEXEXX<u>I</u>XCAN<u>DON'T</u>SEEX<u>KNOW</u>XIXX<u>DON'T</u>X<u>KNOW</u>
HEXSHEX<u>I'M</u>XX<u>SORRY</u>X<u>I</u>JUSTXX<u>DON'T</u>XC<u>KNOW</u>XXXX

Harry Helpless: EXCUSEMEBUT<u>DO</u>XX<u>YOU</u>PERHAPSXXX<u>KNOW</u>XXWE
DOES<u>DO</u>HE<u>YOU</u>YXC<u>KNOW</u>WHEN<u>HOW</u><u>THIS</u><u>WORKS</u>

Young woman: LOOK<u>FIRST</u><u>YOU</u>MUST<u>DO</u><u>B</u><u>THIS</u>BUT<u>AND</u>X<u>THEN</u>HE
WE<u>X</u><u>YOU</u>XX<u>DO</u>XITEXACTLYT<u>THAT</u>XNOWXWATCHMEXC

Harry Helpless: OHXIXSEEX<u>FIRST</u>XXTHE<u>I</u>XMUSTX<u>DO</u>XX<u>THIS</u>XX<u>AND</u>X
ANDXXX<u>THEN</u>XAFTERWARDSXXX<u>I</u>MUSTXX<u>DO</u>X<u>THAT</u>X
COULDXWOULDX<u>CAN</u>XX<u>YOU</u>XXNOWX<u>PLEASE</u>XXXCCC

GIVEXITX<u>SHOW</u>XITXXTOXXX<u>ME</u><u>X</u><u>ONE</u><u>MORE</u>X<u>TIME</u>XXC

Youngwomen: NOWXLOOKXXMAN<u>FIRST</u>XX<u>YOU</u>XMUSTX<u>DO</u>XX<u>THIS</u>XX
NOW<u>AND</u>XAFTERWARDS<u>THEN</u>XX<u>YOU</u>CAN<u>DO</u>X<u>THIS</u>XCC

Harry Helpless: OIXREALLYX<u>THANK</u>XAPPRECIATE<u>YOUR</u>XASSISTANCEX
VERYXMUCH<u>FOR</u>XHISXHERXX<u>YOUR</u>XX<u>HELP</u>XCVVCCC

Young women: OTHISXISQUITEXXALRIGHTX<u>NO</u>THINGX<u>PROBLEM</u>THIS
HISHEROOUR<u>MY</u>X<u>TIME</u><u>PLEASURE</u>XANYXTIMEXXBYEX

Questions (page 72)

1. b,d
2. a,c,d
3. a,c,d
4. a

18: You're Drinking My Strawberry Shake

Balloons (page 74)

I'm sorry, but you took my tray by mistake.

Don't raise your voice to me.

Jumbles (page 75)

Spiderwoman: Excuse me, I'm sorry to tell you
but you took my plate by mistake.
Excuse me, I'm sorry to tell you,
you're eating my strawberry cake.

King Strong: I'm not.

Spiderwoman: You are.

King Strong: Don't get upset. Don't raise your voice.

Spiderwoman: Who is?

King Strong: You are.

Spiderwoman: Please don't raise your voice to me.

Puzzle (page 76)

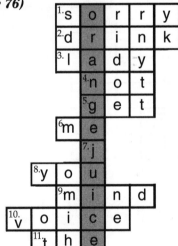

19: Surprise Party

Puzzles (page 78)

SUN + C + FLOWER + HAT − H − CAR − SNOW = U F L E T = F L U T E

= | F | L | U | T | E |

BOTLLE + APPLE − PT − BELL + OF + FINGER − FEET − FROG = O A P I N = PIANO

= | P | I | A | N | O |

Fill–Ins (page 79)

When Larry reached <u>his</u> house at seven

Max was <u>playing</u> his guitar.

Jane was <u>sitting</u> on the table

eating pickles from a <u>jar</u>.

Mark was sitting at the <u>piano</u>

playing <u>sonatas</u> for Louise.

And <u>his</u> parrot Paul was singing

all the tunes and <u>melodies</u>.

Bob <u>was sleeping under</u> the table;

he couldn't even <u>stay awake</u>.

And <u>his</u> dog was in the kitchen

eating up the <u>birthday cake</u>.

Complete (page 80)

Her husband was <u>painting the kitchen</u>.

The baby was <u>sleeping</u>.

Her son Billy was <u>doing a headstand</u>.

Grandma Holmes was <u>reading a book</u>.

Her daughter Lily was <u>playing the guitar</u>.

Fred the dog was <u>dancing</u>.

20: I Miss You So My Dear

Puzzles (page 83)

A:

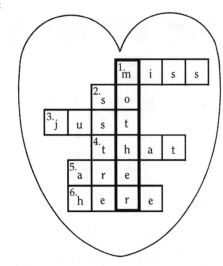

B:

T + ELEPHANT − ANT + ONE = T + ELEPH + ONE =

| T | E | L | E | P | H | O | N | E |

George was surprised because Keiko's <u>mother</u> was on the <u>telephone</u>.
                        A   *B*

Complete (page 84)

She <u>misses</u> you my dear.

She <u>wishes</u> you were here.

She <u>wishes</u> you were here.

She <u>wishes</u> you were here.

She <u>misses</u> you my dear.

She <u>wishes</u> you were here.

She <u>loves</u> you just the way your are.

She <u>loves</u> you just the way you are.

Crazy, or blue, or mad.

She <u>loves</u> you just the way you are.

She <u>loves</u> you just the way you are.

Crazy, or blue, or mad.

She <u>hopes</u> you love her too.

as much as she loves you,

as much as she loves you,

as much as she loves you.

She <u>hopes</u> you love her too,

as much as she loves you.

She <u>hopes</u> you love her too.

21: Sorry You Had to Wait

Grammarhyme (page 86)

Oh, my Penny Sue,

I'm glad to see <u>you</u>.

Sorry you had to wait.

Couldn't help being <u>late</u>.

My bicycle broke down.

I had to walk to <u>town</u>.

Please forgive me. I'm so sorry.

Oh, my Willy dear,

I'm glad that you're <u>here</u>.

I didn't mind the wait.

You're just an hour <u>late</u>.

You don't have to say you're sorry.

Balloons (page 87)

Picture 1: Hi, Roy. I'm <u>glad</u> <u>to</u> <u>see</u> you.

Picture 2: <u>Sorry</u> <u>you</u> <u>had</u> to wait. I couldn't <u>help</u> <u>being</u> <u>late</u>.

Picture 3: My stupid <u>bike</u> <u>broke</u> <u>down</u>. I <u>couldn't</u> <u>ride</u> <u>to</u> <u>town</u>.

Picture 4: Please <u>forgive</u> <u>me</u>. I'm <u>so</u> <u>sorry</u>.

Picture 5: Dear Ted, I'm <u>glad</u> <u>to</u> <u>see</u> <u>you</u> too.

Picture 6: I didn't <u>mind</u> <u>the</u> <u>wait</u>. <u>You're</u> <u>just</u> two hours <u>late</u>.

Picture 7: <u>It's</u> <u>only</u> forty degrees, and <u>I</u> <u>don't</u> <u>mind</u> the rain.

Picture 8: You <u>don't</u> <u>have</u> <u>to</u> <u>say</u> <u>you're</u> <u>sorry</u>.

Balloons (page 88)

(Possible answers)

Balloon 1: Please forgive me, I'm so sorry.

Balloon 2: Don't raise your voice to me.

Balloon 3: I'm so glad to see you.

22: I Just Want My Money Back

Jumbles (page 90)

Sir, could I please get my money back.

This white plate I bought has got a crack.

I paid you by check. Here's my receipt.

My passport's right here. My name's Joe Reed.

The price on it was $12.98.

If you give me cash that would be great.

I just want my cash, just the cash.

I just want my money back.

2. I want to return this <u>suitcase</u>. The <u>handle is broken</u>.
   _a   _b
   I'd like to get <u>my money back</u>.
        _c

3. <u>I want to return this TV</u>. The <u>picture is no good</u>.
       _a   _b
   Can I have <u>another one</u>?
        _c

4. <u>I want to return this cat</u>. It <u>doesn't catch mice</u>.
       _a   _b
   Could I please get <u>my money back</u>?
        _c

Complete (page 91)

1. I want to return this <u>shirt</u>. It's <u>too small</u>. Just look at that.
          _a   _b
   Can I have a <u>larger one</u>?
        _c

Write (page 92)

1. Sir, I would like my money back.

2. This plate I bought has got a crack.

3. Here is my receipt.

Review

Detective (page 94)

1. Miss, I'm looking for a raincoat—not too short, not too long.

2. Hello, please have a seat. What would you like to eat?

3. I come from San Francisco. I'm flying to Peking.

4. I can't seem to find my key. Have you seen my key?

5. It's been so long since we last met. It's been at least a year, I bet.

6. Excuse me, I'm sorry to tell you but you took my drink by mistake.

7. When I reached my house at seven, Max was playing the guitar.

8. I love you so my dear. I wish that you were here.

9. Sorry you had to wait. Couldn't help being late.

10. Miss, could I please have my money back? This teacup I bought has got a crack.

Jumbles (page 96)

1. How much is the sweater in the center window? "I'm Looking For A Raincoat"

2. Would you like your steak well-done? "What Would You Like To Eat?"

3. What are you going to do there? "I'm Leaving For Peking"

4. Can't you see I've looked and looked. "Where's My Key?"

5. It's really great to see you. "Small Talk"

6. Let's let the manager say who's right. "You're Drinking My Strawberry Shake"

7. Jane was sitting on the table eating pickles from a jar. "Surprise Party"

8. I love you just the way you are. "I Miss You So My Dear"

9. You don't have to say you're sorry. "Sorry You Had To Wait"

10. If you gave me cash that would be fine. "I Just Want My Money Back"

Index of Structures

The following index lists the number of the units in which a structure appears several times. It is not a comprehensive listing of all structures in the text or of all occurrences of each structure. The numbers in boldface indicate the unit(s) in which that structure is emphasized.